SEVERNSIDE

A GUIDE TO FAMILY WALKS

SEVERNSIDE
A Guide to Family Walks

Edited by STEPHEN TAYLOR

CROOM HELM LONDON

Printed in Great Britain
by Redwood Burn Ltd, Trowbridge and Esher

CONTENTS

Editor's Foreword
Acknowledgements

SEVERNSIDE   13

1   AN ESTUARY STROLL (4½ miles)   17
    Portishead – Clevedon

2   PORTBURY AND THE FAILAND DOWNS (6 miles)   21
    Portbury – Wraxall Hill – Failand – Portbury

3   A WALK IN BRISTOL'S LAKE DISTRICT (8 miles or 6 miles) 25
    Chew Valley Lake – Compton Martin – Ubley – Chew
    Valley Lake (or Chew Stoke)

4   OVER THE MENDIP CREST TO CHEDDAR (7 miles or   29
    5½ miles)
    Churchill Gate (or Shipham) – Beacon Batch – Cheddar

5   A SOUTHERN MENDIPS WALK FROM WELLS (8 miles)   35
    Wells – Wookey Hole – Ebbor Gorge – Pen Hill – Wells

6   LYMPSHAM AND BRENT KNOLL (4½ miles)   39
    Lympsham – East Brent – Brent Knoll

7   THE BRIDGWATER AND TAUNTON CANAL (7½ miles,   45
    10½ miles, or 14½ miles)
    Bridgwater – Huntworth – Durston – Creech St Michael –
    Taunton

8   THE SOUTHERN QUANTOCKS (9½ miles, 8¾ miles or 6¾   49
    miles)
    Nether Stowey – Over Stowey – Quantock Combe –
    Crowcombe – Aisholt Common – Pepper Hill

9   THE NORTHERN QUANTOCKS (6 miles)   57
    Holford – Black Hill – Beacon Hill – Holford

10   NEWTON PARK AND STANTONBURY (5½ miles or 9 miles) 61
Newton St Loe – Stanton Prior – Compton Dando –
Keynsham

11   GREAT ELM, MURDER COMBE AND NUNNEY (8½ miles) 67
Spring Gardens – Great Elm – Whatley – Nunney – Egford –
Spring Gardens

12   BUCKLAND DINHAM AND ORCHARDLEIGH (9 miles)   71
Buckland Dinham – Spring Gardens – Oldford – Orchardleigh
– Buckland Dinham

13   THE KENNET AND AVON CANAL (4½ miles or 9 miles)   77
Bradford-on-Avon – Avoncliff – Limpley Stoke – Bath

14   LITTLE SOLSBURY HILL AND ST CATHERINE'S   83
VALLEY (7 miles or 3½ miles)
Batheaston – Little Solsbury Hill – St Catherine's –
Batheaston

15   CASTLE COMBE (9 miles)   87
North Wraxall – West Kington – Castle Combe – Ford –
North Wraxall

16   MAUD HEATH'S CAUSEWAY FROM CHIPPENHAM   91
(9 miles)
Chippenham – Wick Hill – East Tytherton – Kellaways –
Chippenham

17   DURSLEY, STINCHCOMBE HILL AND THE TYNDALE   95
MONUMENT (7¼ miles)
Dursley – Stinchcombe Hill – North Nibley – Dursley

18   WOTTON-UNDER-EDGE, KINGSWOOD AND   101
BLACKQUARRIES HILL (6 miles)

19   RODBOROUGH COMMON AND THE GOLDEN VALLEY 105
(4 miles)
Stroud – Brimscombe – Rodborough Common – Stroud

20   CRANHAM AND THE HILL ABOVE PARADISE   111
      (9 miles or 5 miles)
      Witcombe — Cranham — Painswick Beacon — Cooper's Hill
      — Witcombe

21   THE MALVERN HILLS AND COMMONS (8½ miles)   117
      Coombegreen Common — Herefordshire Beacon —
      Midsummer Hill — Chase End Hill — Camer's Green

22   FRAMPTON-ON-SEVERN (5½ miles or 3 miles)   121
      Claypits Hill — Frampton-on-Severn — Claypits Hill

23   A SEVERN PENINSULAR WALK (6½ miles)   127
      Frampton Bridge — Fretherne — Barrow Hill — Upper
      Framilode — Saul — Frampton Bridge

24   MAY HILL AND NEWENT WOODS (4 miles)   131
      Dursley Cross — May Hill — Clifford's Mesne — Newent
      Woods — Dursley Cross

25   THE LOWER WYE AND OFFA'S DYKE (9 miles or 5 miles)   135
      Chepstow — Tintern Abbey — Wyndcliff — Chepstow

26   TO THE KYMIN AND INTO THE FOREST OF DEAN   141
      (7 miles)
      Redbrook — The Kymin — Staunton — Newland — Redbrook

27   A GWENT GEM (7 miles)   145
      Llangwm — Wolvesnewton — Llansoy — Llangwm

The Contributors   148

The Commons, Open Spaces and Footpaths Preservation Society 150

The Ramblers' Association   151

The Countryside Commission   152

Bus and Train Enquiry Points   153

Principal Sources of Tourist Information   154

EDITOR'S FOREWORD

When did you last enjoy a real country walk? If you set about it the right way it is the finest and cheapest way to experience at close quarters the myriad delights of the countryside. In the lovely area of Severnside we have inherited from our forebears a marvellous network of public footpaths which can take us — if we so choose — well off the beaten track to wind-swept hilltops, remote hamlets, deep forests, ruined castles and peaceful waterways.

If you need any guidance or ideas on where to walk, this book is for you. Here are 27 very varied walks, some short and some a little more ambitious, written with care and devotion by people who have a special knowledge of the area and a deep feeling for it; and in describing some of the fascinating features of each walk they have tried to impart the personal touch. We hope that as you read through you will catch their enthusiasm and decide to try out these walks yourself.

A special feature of these walks is that they can all be reached by bus or train (even though in some cases a little ingenuity may be required!). These are difficult days for public transport, however, and no guarantee can be given that the services indicated at the head of each walk will necessarily be operating in the same way by the time you come to plan your walk. So please check carefully before you set out. A list of the appropriate bus and train enquiry points is given at the end of the book. Of course, it goes without saying that the walks can also be enjoyed by anyone coming by car; details of parking facilities are given wherever possible.

If you are not used to much walking it would be as well to put in a little practice before attempting any of the more ambitious routes; and to wear sensible boots or shoes which have been properly broken in. Blistered feet can be agonising! Take your time and look around; there is so much to see. If you are averaging 2 m.p.h. you are not doing at all badly.

Although these walks use public rights of way please remember that they are over privately owned land, from which the farmer is making his living, and that you are there as a guest. Also, it is worth bearing in mind that all country walks are subject to changes as the seasons wear on; so if you undertake any of these walks some considerable time after they have been published it would be sensible to check that the paths still exist or are usable.

Finally, enjoy your walks – and please remember the Country Code:

Guard against all risk of fire
Fasten all gates
Keep dogs under proper control
Keep to the paths across farm land
Avoid damaging fences, hedges and walls
Leave no litter – take it home
Safeguard water supplies
Protect wild life, wild plants and trees
Go carefully on country roads
Respect the life of the countryside

S.P.T.

The publishers disclaim all responsibility for any loss, damage or injury to property or persons, however caused, on any of the walks described in this book.

ACKNOWLEDGEMENTS

I am indebted to a number of people who have helped and advised me in the production of this book. I particularly wish to thank Fred Whitwood for much practical help given with the field-work which has been involved, Irene Abbotts for her valiant performance on the type-writer, and my wife for her great forbearance and unfailing support, without which the project would not have been possible.

The Illustrations: John Abbotts has based most of his drawings on actual photographs, and the publishers wish to thank the following photographers for permission to have their copyright work reproduced: Dennis Thoms (Walk 2); Geoffrey N. Wright (Walk 9); Harold Overton (Walks 10 and 14); Derrick Boorne (Walk 21); Stephen Taylor (Walks 1, 3, 4, 7, 11, 12, 16, 17, 18, 19, 20, 22, 23, 24). (Crown Copyright – Walk 25.)

All the Ordnance Survey maps reproduced are Crown Copyright.

S.P.T.

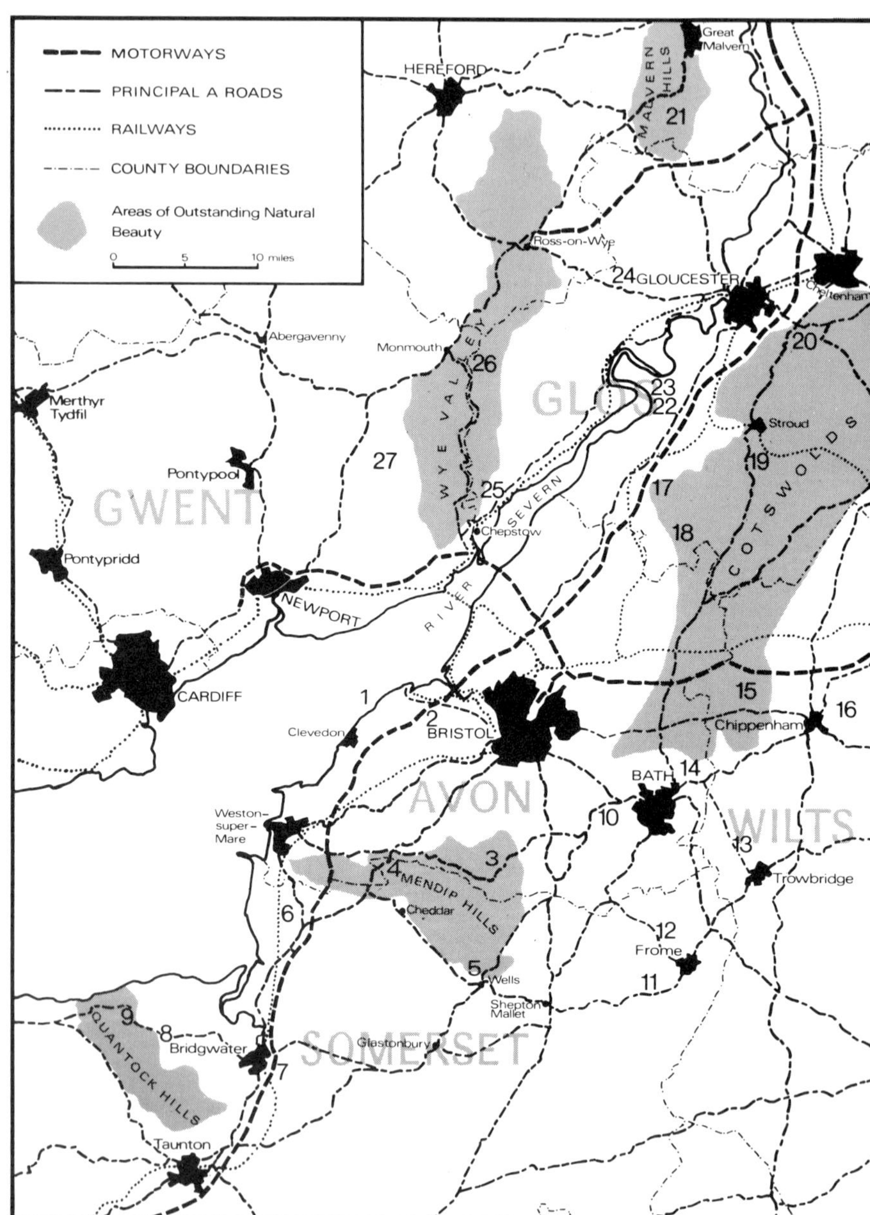

MOTORWAYS
PRINCIPAL A ROADS
RAILWAYS
COUNTY BOUNDARIES
Areas of Outstanding Natural Beauty
0 5 10 miles
HEREFORD
Great Malvern
MALVERN HILLS
21
Ross-on-Wye
24 GLOUCESTER
Cheltenham
Abergavenny
Monmouth
26
20
Merthyr Tydfil
GLOS
23
22
Stroud
Pontypool
27
WYE VALLEY
19
GWENT
25
17
COTSWOLDS
Chepstow
18
SEVERN
Pontypridd
NEWPORT
RIVER
15
CARDIFF
1
16
Clevedon
2
Chippenham
BRISTOL
AVON
BATH
14
Weston-super-Mare
10
WILTS
3
13
4
MENDIP HILLS
6
Cheddar
Trowbridge
5
12
Frome
Wells
11
Shepton Mallet
9
QUANTOCK HILLS
8
Bridgwater
7
SOMERSET
Glastonbury
Taunton

SEVERNSIDE

Stephen Taylor

For want of a better title I have called the area covered by these walks Severnside, after its most notable physical feature — Britain's longest river. It is not a strictly accurate title, of course, because the area extends beyond that to take in the Malvern Hills, part of north-west Wiltshire and the area around Frome in Somerset. Moreover, it excludes South Wales apart from a brief venture across the Welsh border to include a little of Gwent. It contains a very high proportion of immensely attractive country of great variety and interest. It includes in fact no less than five officially designated Areas of Outstanding Natural Beauty — the Quantock Hills, the Mendip Hills, the Wye Valley, the Malvern Hills and the Cotswolds. Apart from Bristol there are no really large built-up areas. It is ideal country for the walker.

Much of its beauty derives from its complex geological character and history — the folding and tilting of the rocks, the laying down over vast periods of time of the beds which form the basis of much of the landscape, and the tremendous eroding forces of water and ice over immense periods of time which have carved and shaped them into their present forms. Amongst its attractive geological features are the warm, red, fertile soils of Somerset and parts of Gloucestershire, the striking outline of the Malverns, composed of very ancient pre-Cambrian rocks, rising abruptly above the Vale of Evesham like a range of small mountains, the steep scarp of the limestone Cotswolds and isolated hills such as May Hill (sandstone) and Brent Knoll (limestone and shale) sprinkled about the flat plains to add interest and provide remarkable viewpoints.

In fact most of these walks feature a viewpoint of some kind or another — it is that kind of country. As you try out a fresh walk the urge to identify old familiar landmarks from a new angle can become irresistible. You look for viewpoints from viewpoints — 'I'm sure that's the Tyndale Monument.' or 'What's that line of hills in the distance on the right? Is it the Quantocks?' — and so on. It is well worth spending some time on these heights with a pair of binoculars and a map getting to know where all the hills are and how they relate to each other and to the valleys below. No geography lesson could be more pleasant or more rewarding.

Man has inhabited this area from earliest times and has left his mark

on it, though happily not so disastrously as in other parts of the
country. On the Mendips there was once extensive lead mining and
smelting. In the Forest of Dean iron was once mined and large numbers
of oaks were cut down to provide fuel to smelt it, until the competing
demands of the Navy for Warship construction put a stop to that
practice. There is coal here too, and in the area south-west of Bath;
mining of that still goes on. Another important industry has always
been that of quarrying. The area is noted for its fine-quality building
stone which gives great character and charm to so many of its towns
and villages. The production of wool and the weaving of cloth was the
industry which brought prosperity to the Cotswolds. As demand increased more and more mills sprang up along the valleys with their
swift-flowing streams, and their sites can be seen today.

These walks not only introduce you to the area as it now is, but they
also gently remind you of events which occurred long ago. In fact with
a little imagination you can stir up the ghosts of the past as you absorb
the individual atmosphere of each walk. Here are a few possibilities.

Up on the Quantock ridge can you not visualise Neolithic man
hunting for food or hacking away at the virgin soil of the hilltops with
his feeble tools to construct his burial mounds? Or maybe as you ascend
the wooded slopes of the Cotswolds you can see a group of Roman
workmen constructing a luxury villa in a choice situation, with materials
brought in along the nearby chariotway to Glevum (Gloucester).

Again, high above the Wye Valley near Tintern imagine the cursing
as an army of labourers excavate a great dyke in the stony soil to mark
the boundary of King Offa's domain. Then, down at Wells think what it
must have been like to see the great new cathedral gradually taking
shape, the hovels of its workmen contrasting sadly with its splendour.

At Chippenham picture the homely scene of poor old Maud Heath
getting stuck in the mud on her way to market and vowing to do something about the appalling state of fifteenth-century roads. Not so very
far away, at Nunney, think of the horrors of the Civil War as you con-
template the cannon-shattered walls of the castle. Finally, at Stroud it
is not difficult to imagine the proud moment when the new canal was
opened and the first cargo brought in from the Severn.

That thought brings us back to the source of our title, the mighty
and the mysterious Severn, which at once unifies and separates the
components of our area. Swift and treacherous, sometimes awe-inspiring
when it is topped by its monstrous Bore, it demands our respect, if not
our affection. As we drive in comfort high above it on the Severn
Bridge let us spare a thought for the steel-nerved men who so brilliantly

carried out their task of linking Severnside with — Severnside. Surely nothing in this twentieth century can have had such an impact on the area as this.

Here then is Severnside. A wonderful piece of country lies before you to explore, to savour and to treasure.

AVON (England)
76
75
74
73
72
Black Nore
Nautical Sch
35
Hang Rock
Redcliff Bay
99
P
Charlcombe Bay
Weston Down
Walton Bay
Weston-
in-Gordano
P
Pigeon House Bay
55
Farley
Inn
Walton
Down
Field
System
Enclosure
Hut Circles
Weston
Moor
Margaret's Bay
69
Back Hill
Golf Course
Castle Hill
P
Walton-
in-Gordano
Ladye Point
CH
5
Clapton
Wick
17
Ladye Bay
Castle
(rems of)
Enclosure
Field System
Walton Moor
Walton Park
12
Nortons
Wood
23
Tickenham
Sch
Pier
Dial
Hill
90
The Warren
Court Hill
Clevedon Bay
The Park
NT
Field System
Clevedon
Court
22 MS
CLEVEDON
23
Cadbury Court
Fm
Littleharp Bay
East
Clevedon
Land Yeo
Salthouse Bay
Tickenham Moor
Vain
Hill
Church
Hill
7
Pottery
Clevedon
Moor
5
Wks
5
Nailsea Moor

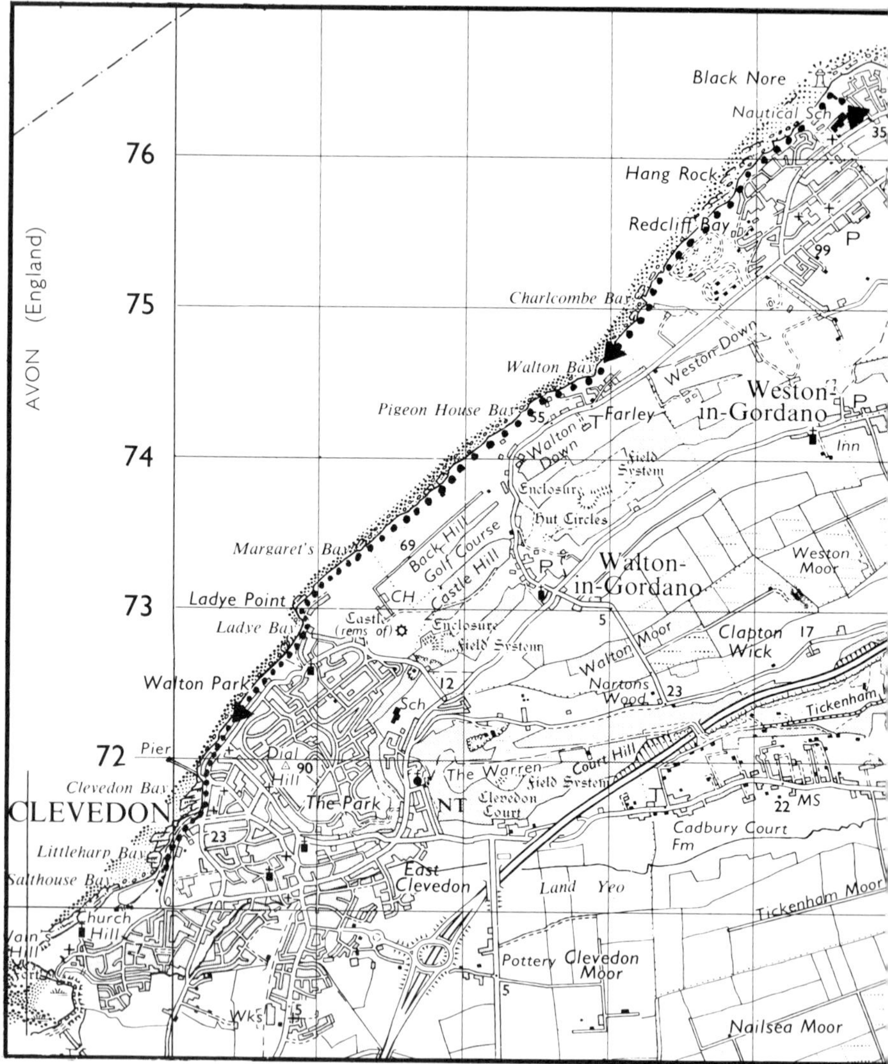

O.S. 172

1 AN ESTUARY STROLL (4½ miles)

Ian Campbell

*Travel: Bristol Bus No. 358/359 Bristol – Portishead. Service every 20
mins. weekdays, hourly Sundays. Return by Bristol Bus No. 362/363
Clevedon – Bristol. Half-hourly service, hourly Sundays.
[Map: Ordnance Survey 1:50,000 Series, Sheet 172.]*

This is a walk for a short winter day — or perhaps a summer evening
when the tide is in.

Stay on the bus through Portishead to its suburb of Redcliffe Bay.
Make your way down to the coast path — Nore House, near the lighthouse, or Hillside Road are good access points. The beach and cliff edge
at Redcliffe Bay have been acquired by the National Trust, but the area
here is very densely developed with bungalows and houses of people
working in Bristol or the growing docks at Portishead. Turn left along
the coast path, leaving Portishead and Nore lighthouse behind you.
Prominent on the foreshore is the enormous 'hang rock', which at half
tide looks as though some prehistoric monster is emerging from the
water.

The path is easy to follow here, but the landward view is not very
attractive: a mass of bungalows and caravans and then, for about a
quarter of a mile, a high wire fence enclosing an underground storage
establishment. Seaward, however, is a different matter. The Severn
Estuary is here widening to the open sea. On the far horizon the islands
of Steep Holm and Flat Holm can be seen on clear days and, nearer at
hand, the Welsh coast. It is not difficult to pick out Newport and
even Cardiff in the distance, if visibility is reasonably good. Soon the
storage establishment is passed and open fields come down to the cliff
edge. A delightful little pebbly beach is seen here — Charlcombe Bay,
one of the easier access points to the water. The path passes through a
fairly densely wooded area, and in wet weather this stretch can be
muddy. There is a small caravan site around here, but then no further
human habitation before Clevedon. Soon the path comes out on to the
open cliff and there is a stretch of really superb cliff-top walking. There
are frequent routes down to the rocks — at one stage the rocks are so
flat as to look almost like a man-made promenade. They are in fact a
natural 'platform' just above the high-tide level.

Although this walk is enjoyable at all times, if possible choose a day with high tide during the course of your walk. Tides are all-important on this coast. The Bristol Channel has the second-highest rise and fall of tides in the world — the highest is the similarly shaped Bay of Fundy in Canada. Effectively, most of the ports in the Bristol Channel have until recently been high-tide ports. Bristol itself has never been accessible more than 4 or 5 hours out of every twelve and this was one of the reasons why it had to yield to Liverpool in the eighteenth century as the main west coast port. For this reason, too, all the estuary in front of you — indeed right down channel to Steep Holm island and half-way over to the Welsh coast — has always been historically part of the port of Bristol. This enabled ships to anchor here whilst waiting for a tide to take them up the Avon.

The large rise and fall means a very fast flood tide — and it is fascinating to watch an incoming tide racing up the beaches. When a flood tide has a prevailing south-west wind behind it, the waves can be pretty strong in attacking the cliffs.

After you round a high headland, the battered Clevedon pier comes into view a mile or so away. The end of the pier is quite cut off from the remainder, a central portion having been destroyed when the pier was tested with heavy weights some years ago. Subsequently strong

Ladye Bay, Clevedon

tides and winds increased the damage and it now seems unlikely that the pier will ever be restored. Below you is a fine pebble beach — Ladye Bay — which is popular with bathers in the season. It's worth a descent and a rest here before the final stretch into Clevedon. Ladye Bay, sheltered on the north and east by high cliffs is quite a sun trap and even on winter days can be warm and mild.

The cliff path into Clevedon has a metalled surface and the main front by the pier is soon reached. Bristolians, of course, will know Clevedon, but for visitors from further afield this small Victorian watering place has many points of interest. During the Regency, Clevedon began to flourish as a watering place and many literary figures came to stay and write here, including Coleridge and Tennyson the poets, Thackeray the novelist and Walter Bagehot the constitutional lawyer and writer. In Victorian times Clevedon was overtaken by its brasher neighbour Weston-super-Mare. Indeed, Clevedon has never become a resort at all in the modern sense, but has remained essentially a quiet watering place for the retired and for commuters, with a little light industry, such as Hale's bakery, out on the Bristol road. It remains to be seen whether the coming of the M5 to the outskirts of Clevedon a few years ago will change its character.

There is a half-hourly bus service back to Bristol from the front just beyond the pier beach.

Sheepway
Lodway
Ferry
Pill
14
7
15
P
9
Overhill
P
Priory
(site of)
Earthwork
Portbury
P
36
Easton-in-Gordano
PH
Caswell
Cross
The Mount
Markham
Fm
Range
Prior's
Wood
56
Happerton
Fms
Windmill
120
Hill
97
Charlton Lower
Fm
The Downs
School
Lower
Failand
T
Moat House
Fm
Failand
Ho
Old
Hill
Failand Hill
28
Failand
Fm
149
West Hill
Lodge
Failand
Lodge
159
Wraxall
Court
Earthwork
P
147
Wraxall
52
MP
PH
P
Failand
P
142
Longwood
Ho
Wraxall
Ho
Inn
38
Tyntesfield
3
MP
Lodge
Tyntesfield
Plantn
Ashton Hill
Plantn
48
Land Yeo
MP
Belmont
Ho
87
Gable
Fm

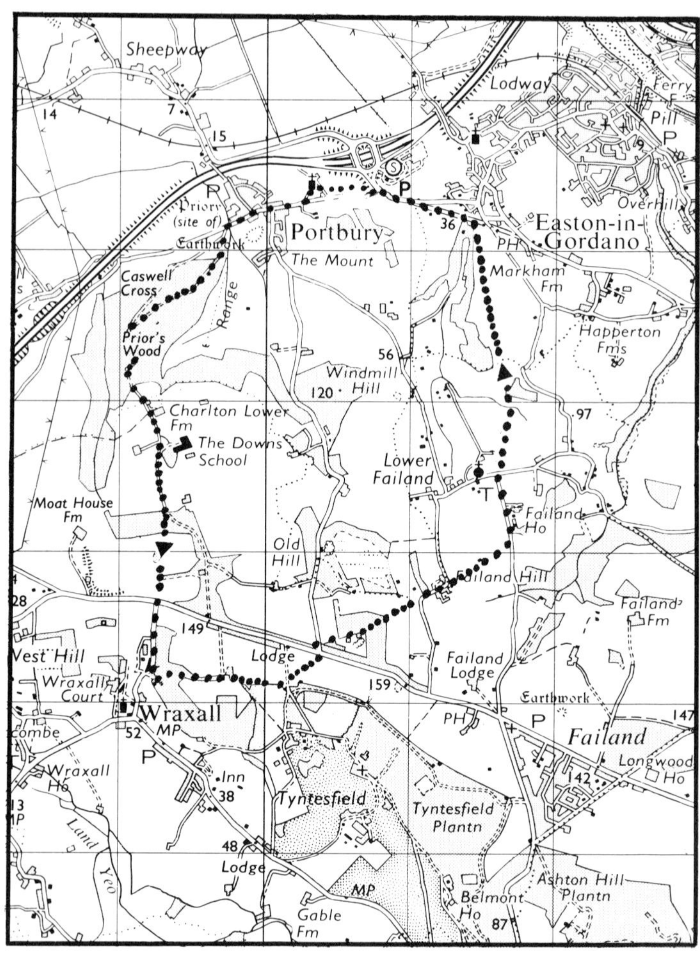

O.S. 172

2 PORTBURY AND THE FAILAND DOWNS (6 miles)

Dennis Thoms

*Travel: Bristol Bus Nos. 358 and 359 from Bristol or Portishead to
Portbury roundabout. Motorists: Park at lay-by south of this rounda-
bout on the A369 (G.R. 507753) or at Gordano Services Area at
Junction 19 on the M5.*
Refreshments: Gordano Services Area; Priory Inn, Portbury.
[Map: Ordnance Survey 1:50,000 Series, Sheet 172.]

As you drive swiftly westwards from Bristol along the M5 you may
sometimes wonder, longingly, what it would be like to be out there in
that peaceful countryside you see on either side. This walk gives you
the chance to find out and to get away from it all for a few hours, even
though you may be no more than 5 miles from the centre of Bristol, as
the crow flies.

At the Portbury roundabout (G.R. 507755) look for a stile and a
footpath thence to Portbury Church, visible to the west. (If you prefer,
you can get to the church by the road running parallel to this path.) The
building dates from the early twelfth century, but there are, of course,
many later additions and alterations. There is also a suggestion that part
of an earlier Saxon building is incorporated in the chancel. The building
is surprisingly large for what appeared to be until recently a very small
community. No doubt when the Berkeley family had a manor nearby
(now demolished) the population would have been much larger.

On leaving the church follow the road westward through the village
towards the Priory, the tall building straight ahead, not to be confused
with the nearby inn bearing the same name. The Priory was established
in the late twelfth century as a small cell of Augustinian canons. The
existing building is probably early fifteenth-century and has been much
altered and reconditioned, particularly in the nineteenth century when
it became part dwelling and part school. It remained as a school until
1972 and then became vacant. (Incidentally, you might like to bear in
mind that the Priory Inn is the only source of refreshments on this
walk, apart from the Services Area.)

A little further on, enter the drive by a lodge to the left of the road,
and select the middle of the three tracks. Soon a cottage is passed on
the left, whilst on the right, where a wood has been felled, there is a
fine open view to Portishead, Avonmouth, and sometimes as far as the

Gwent coast and the Severn Bridge. The track soon enters Priors Wood
and winds up to the plateau separating the Gordano Valley from the
next valley.

After leaving the wood Charlton Lower Farm is passed on the left.
Notice the unusual octagonal building at the south-west corner, with
leaded-light windows. This is a nineteenth-century buttery, fully tiled
inside with marble-slabbed butter-making stations and a central foun-
tain to keep it cool.

Continue south along the drive, past the entrance to Charlton House,
now the Downs School, until the drive starts to bear left and there is a
cottage ahead. Go through a gate on the right-hand side of the drive,
and continue due south, to a gate leading to a wood. Go straight
through the wood, across a field, through the centre of a copse, continuing with the field boundary on your right till you reach the road at
the top of Wraxall Hill. Cross the Tickenham Road (B3128) and go
down Wraxall Hill till the road bends right and there is a track off to the
left. Take this, bear left almost immediately and follow the track
through the wood, bearing right where a path leaves the sunken way
you have been following.

Leaving the wood, follow the left-hand boundary of a field, past a
pair of cottages until a stile is seen at right-angles to the boundary
which has been followed. Beyond this the path is on the north side of a
wall until another stile takes you across a tarmac driveway. Bear left
after crossing the drive and strike diagonally across the field to meet the

Buttery, Charleton Lower Farm

B3128 at the far corner. Cross the road and turn left for a few yards to
the junction with Portbury Lane. A few feet down the lane there is a
gate on the right, and the path hugs the right-hand field boundary, with
quarry buildings beyond it. The path continues more or less in the same
east-north-east direction through a wood, over a stile and along a field
boundary to a gate into a short section of enclosed path terminating in
a stile with a top bar which can be raised. Go through the wicket gate
opposite, down the bank and along the road without substantially
changing direction. Note the bell turret with the copper cupola to the
right of the farmhouse ahead. Follow the bend in the road and enter the
cricket field to walk along its northern boundary, continuing with a
hedge on the left, and cross three stiles until you reach a gate leading
into Oxhouse Lane. Turn left and walk along the road to the T-junction,
where you can if desired divert to visit Failand Church (nineteenth-
century), the spire of which is a prominent landmark. Otherwise continue in a northerly direction over a stile, following the right-hand
hedge to a further stile, and continuing northwards, cross the next field
to a stile in a dip at the bottom. Go down the hill beyond this and up
the other side to cross a stile in the distant left-hand corner. Keep going
in a straight line, over the next stile, then continue with a wood on the
left. Soon there is a wide view towards Bristol and northwards across
the British Channel; the Avon Bridge on the M5 is also prominent. When
the edge of the wood bears away to the left keep a little right of straight,
aiming at the projecting corner of the next field. Here there is another
stile, and you can soon rejoin the edge of the wood to follow it all the
way to the A369, where you turn left to return to the starting place.

Court
Tumulus 134
Howgrove Fm
Regilbury Park Fm
T Ridgehill
ROMAN TEMPLE
(site of)
Highfield
Weir
Pagans Hill
The Oaks
Sch
Long Barrow
Walnut Tree Fm
74
Chew Stoke
P
Butcombe
The Knoll
51
Sage's Fm
Strode
Lower Strode
104
Woodford Hill
Tower
Nempnett Fm
Plaster's Green
118
Gravel Hill
Obelisk
MS
Stoke Villice
Denny Island
West Town
Highlands
150
136
132
Chew Va
Lake
Nempnett Thrubwell
T
Rugmoor Fm
PH
Breach Hill
ROMAN VILLA
(site of)
on Lake
Ubley Park Ho
Herons Green
P
MS 55
Holt Fm
Woodbridge Fm
Moat
Snatch Ho
Bickfield Fm
ROMAN ROAD
Herriotts Br
64
Ubley
P
Rookery Fm
105
Lower Gu Fm
Ubley Hill Fm
Cleve Hill
75
80
Blue Bowl Inn
White Cross Fm
Tumuli
Compton Wood
Compton Martin
West Harptree
Inn
P
263
Hazel Fm
Brownings Tump
The Wrangle
119
P
84
Warren Fm
Home Fm
PH
195
Ridge
Beaconfield Fm
Cemy
P
River Ch

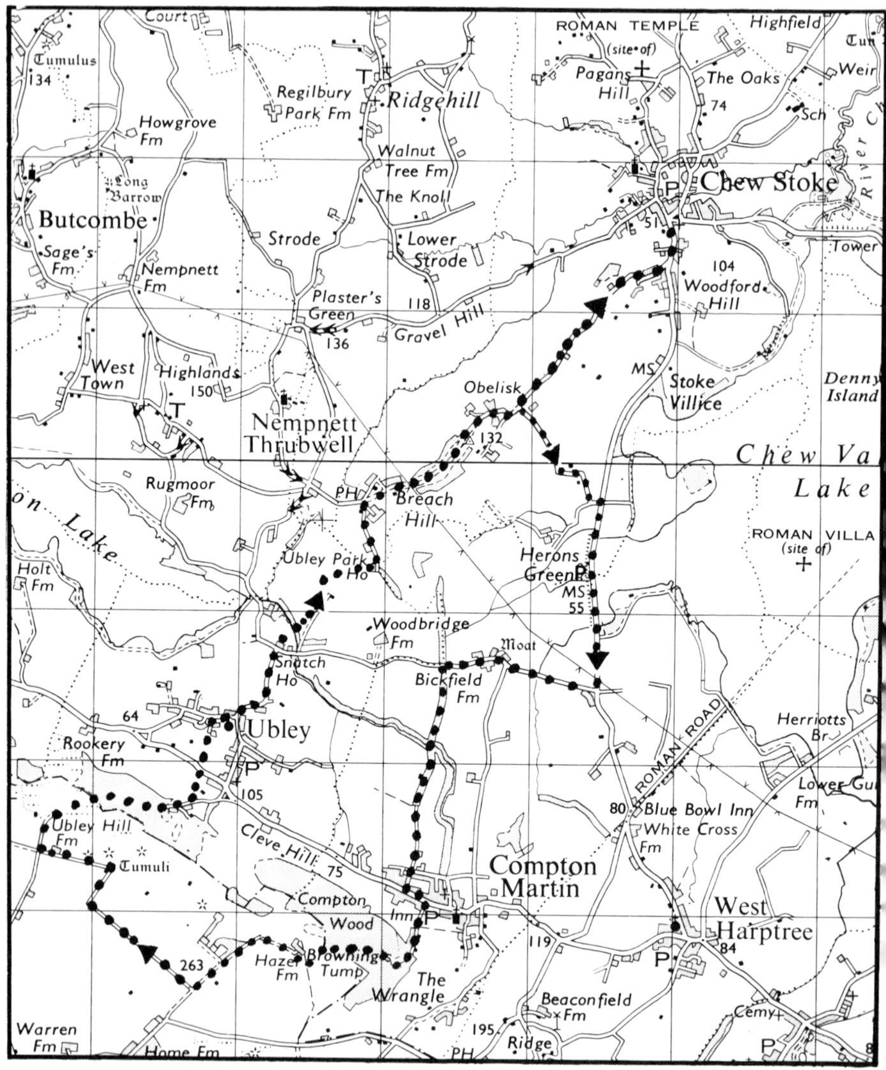

O.S. 172

3 A WALK IN BRISTOL'S LAKE DISTRICT (8 miles if you use your car; 6 miles if you use buses)

Kenneth Pinnock

This is an easy and straightforward ramble through the delectable countryside situated between the Chew Valley Lake and Blagdon Lake, the two big reservoirs for the Bristol area.

Travel: From Bristol Bus Station, Bristol Bus Nos. 374 and 375 to Compton Martin (weekdays only). Return to Bristol from Chew Stoke by same service. Motorists: Ample parking alongside the Chew Valley Lake between Chew Stoke and West Harptree on B3114.
Refreshments: Available in Compton Martin and at the Bell Inn at Ubley.
[Map: Ordnance Survey 1:50,000 Series, Sheet 172 or 182.]

From the Lake car park go along the B3114 in the direction of West Harptree until you come to the Ubley turn. Turn right along here for three-quarters of a mile, passing historic Moat Farm on your right, to a green track on the left just past some electricity transformers. This track showed signs of recent clearance work when this walk was prepared, and the banks were massed with a profusion of wild flowers. After the first crossing track, which connects the fields on each side, the track became rougher, necessitating taking the left bank as an alternative to walking in the deep trench. If you find the going has not materially improved you may prefer to go into the right-hand field and follow parallel to the proper track, which you can rejoin over a stile at the end. Climb the facing stile to enter an area of trees, bearing left on the path, which at first runs between a hedge on the left and a deep ditch. Soon, on leaving the cover of the trees, the track opens out and becomes a pleasant rutted country lane leading straight into the pretty village of Compton Martin. Turn left along the main street, past the Ring o'Bells public house. If you have taken the bus from Bristol to this village, this is where you join the walk.

From the Ring o'Bells and continuing in the same direction, take the first turning right along a lane rising up to Compton Wood. Passing the last cottage on the left, ignore the more obvious track going straight ahead, and follow instead the narrower one immediately to the right near a gate. This track rises sharply just inside this wood, to give ever-widening views over the village and the two lakes beyond. Veer left opposite the iron stile soon encountered, and follow the track ahead through the wood, as it climbs steadily and then emerges into an open field at G.R. 536567. Bear slightly left up to Hazel Farm, passing through the gate on your right next to a barn, into the farmyard. Turn left almost immediately between farm buildings to leave obviously via another gate. Now follow the farm service road, bearing left over a cattle grid and so straight on through an avenue of trees. Notice the tall slender mast of the Television Station on Pen Hill, 5½ miles away on the left. About half a mile after the farm turn right through an open gateway along a stony track and follow it for about 1½ miles to a crossing track at a house (G.R. 516574). Here turn right, soon descending along a clear path through a wood towards Ubley. Bear left along a minor road after the path ends, then climb a stone stile in the left wall half-way down the hill, to enter a large field. Go straight across this to a gate on the far side, opening on to the A368 (G.R. 527580). Cross over the road slightly left and enter a field over a low stile in the hedge, and follow the right hedge straight into Ubley, opposite the school. Turn right to the church at the road junction and the stepped village cross, which looks much older than it is. The church contains a very old chained Bible, and there are no pews, only humble little chairs. (A nearby inscription explains why.)

Leave Ubley by the Nempnett/Chew Stoke road, which you follow to its T-junction in half a mile. Here take the footpath straight ahead to enter a field over a stile immediately left of the house opposite. Keep to the right hedge, climb two stiles in quick succession, and so enter a second field, which you now cross to two large gates, one on each side of a bridge over the stream at G.R. 534589. We now need to get to Ubley Park House. But the map is now very misleading, as it shows a track which in fact quickly peters out in the field, and a building at G.R. 536591 which does not exist. Close attention to the following instructions is therefore essential. From the bridge just mentioned, walk the length of the field to a facing large field gate near the right corner. Go through this and continue in the same direction through a second field and to another field gate in the facing hedge, climbing fairly steeply. Go through this gate and cross the third field, climbing more steeply still and making for two gates in the top corner set at right-angles to each other. Ubley Park House will be seen on the right, and you reach it by climbing over the right-hand gate and then following the left hedge to a white-painted stile and gate in the facing fence. Follow the track left, to join a made-up service road, via a

Ubley Church

galvanised gate. Turn left straight along the road to Breach Hill Farm at G.R. 539597. Turn right here and walk 2 miles straight along the minor road to Chew Stoke where you can get your bus back to Bristol.

If, however, you have come by car and parked where suggested at the side of Chew Valley Lake, follow the same road, but after about 1 mile, just before the Bristol Water Works obelisk, turn right on to another minor road. This eventually comes out to the B3114, where you turn right to the car park.

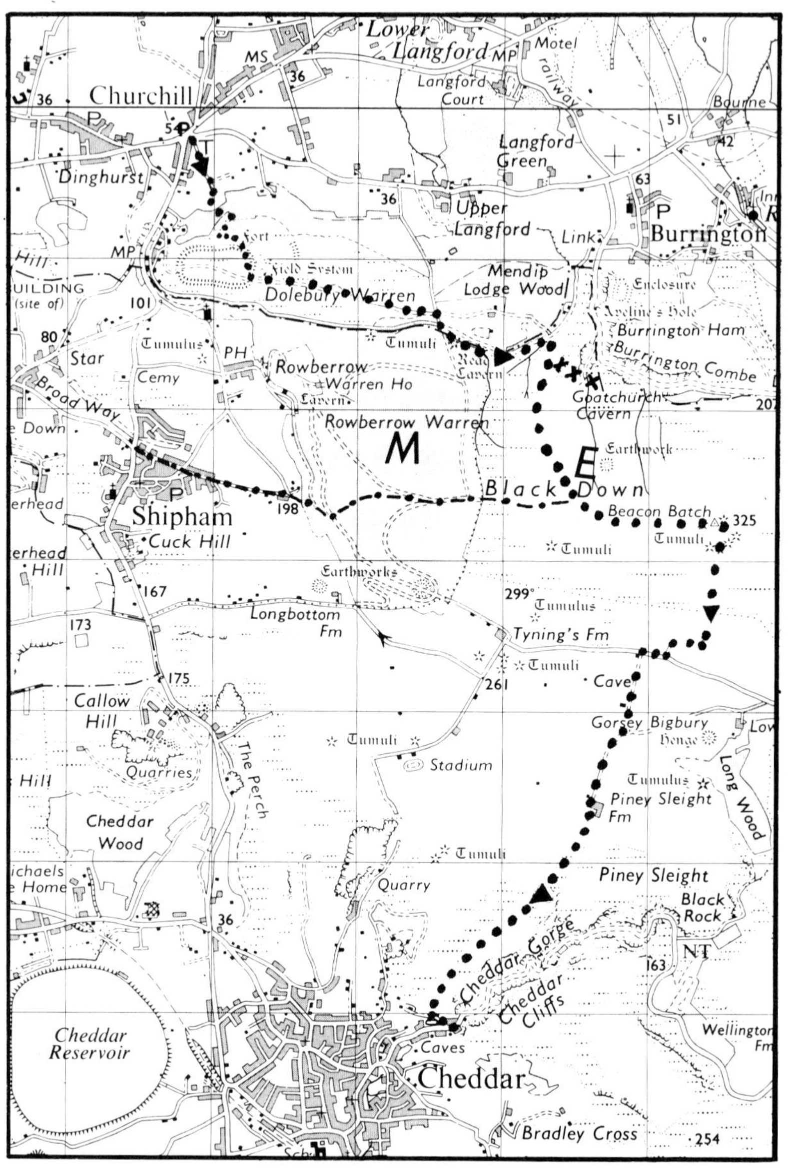

O.S. 182   ✗✗✗✗ diversion   •━•━• shorter walk

4 OVER THE MENDIP CREST TO CHEDDAR (7 miles; shorter route 5½ miles)

Ian Campbell

Travel: Bristol Bus No. 369 or 370 from Bristol to Churchill Gate. Hourly weekdays, infrequent Sundays. Return by Bristol bus No. 370 from Cheddar to Bristol. Approximately two-hourly service. Motorists: Can park near Churchill Gate and return by bus from Cheddar. Refreshments: Ample facilities in Cheddar.
[Map: Ordnance Survey 1:50,000 Series, Sheet 182.]

The hamlet of Churchill, where this walk commences, was the original home of the ancestors of Sir Winston Churchill. From here John Churchill went to the Courts of Charles II and James II, made his fortune as soldier and courtier and was subsequently ennobled as Duke of Marlborough. Ironically, one of his first great battles was against men from his own county, when he commanded James II's army against the Somerset rebels led by the Duke of Monmouth at the battle of Sedgemoor, some twenty miles to the south.

Alight from the bus at Churchill Gate and take the farm road which splits the angle formed by the A38 to Bridgwater and A368 to Bath. This is a private metalled track with public right of way on foot. At the approach to the farmhouse a sign is seen, 'Footpath to Dolebury Warren'. The path leaves the farm access on the right but then bends left round the back of the house and ascends the hill. After a while the path joins a broad track. Turn right on to this and follow it as it makes a horseshoe bend, slowly ascending. About some couple of hundred yards past the bend, look out for a path leading upwards by a V-turn on your right. This is steep, and somewhat overgrown, but easily passable. After a sharp climb, the path emerges suddenly at Dolebury Camp – an Iron Age fortification with massive stone walls built in the first century BC. In the years before the Roman conquest there was almost continuous inter-tribal warfare, and this fort would have been an excellent defensive stronghold. It is believed that the fort may have been re-occupied by the Britons some five centuries later during the so-called Dark Ages when the Saxons were advancing into the West Country.

The site which provided Celtic tribesmen with a dominating view of their enemies' movements provides the modern walker with a breath-taking panoramic view of Mendip peaks: Wavering Down and Crook

Peak to the south-west, Fry's Hill to the south and massive Blackdown
to the south-east. Some dozen miles or so to the west are the waters of
the Bristol Channel and, on clear days, the Welsh coast on the horizon.
A mile or so south, surrounded on all sides by the hills, is the village of
Shipham, starting point for the alternative, shorter route.

Leave the hill fort by its eastern exit and follow the track along the
crest of Dolebury Warren. When the track forks, take the right-hand
one, which gradually converges with the line of the huge Forestry
Commission woodland of Rowberrow Warren. The path descends to a
stile. Cross this and turn right for a few yards along a wide and well-
trodden track. At the junction of tracks take the left one which goes
through thick bracken and then follows the boundary of a wood on
your left. Shortly after this path becomes stony, turn right on to a wide
bridleway which is clearly visible climbing upwards towards the top of
the Mendips. On the left, the cliffs of Burrington Combe can be seen.
It was these cliffs which inspired the Rev. Augustus Toplady, Rector of
Blagdon in the 1760s, to write the hymn 'Rock of Ages, Cleft for me'.
Our route continues up to the crest, but the adventuresome may like a
small, but very rough diversion to Goatchurch Cavern. Leave the main
bridleway by a path on the left through dense bracken. This soon
descends by a very steep climb of some 40 feet or so into a small narrow
valley. Clamber up the other side, ignore the first, very small opening
and about halfway up the slope is the main entrance to Goatchurch
Cavern. This stretches some 500 yards or so downwards into the hillside and is one of the innumerable caves underneath the Mendips, cut
out by water percolating through the cracks in the limestone. The
angle of the entrance is such that natural light enables one to go some
50 or 60 yards in quite easily and safely, but those without experience
of caving should not venture further. There are no sheer drops, but the
floor of the cave, which descends quite steeply, can be very slippery.
Goatchurch Cavern is used as a 'beginners' cave' for those taking up the
sport of caving.

Return from Goatchurch to the bridleway and continue an exhilar-
ating climb upwards. Pause every now and again to turn and look at the
panorama opening behind you. Dolebury, which seemed so high when
you were standing on its top a short while ago, now appears to be a
relatively little hill. A long stretch of coastline, with the prominent
headlands of Brean Down, Worlebury, Sandpoint and Clevedon is
clearly visible. Near the top, take a narrow track off half left, tramping
through the heather. This is around the 1000-foot contour (or perhaps
one has to say 300-odd metres). Soon the path joins the broad wide

track on the crest itself, running eastward between two lines of piles of turf. These were hastily thrown up in the Second World War, to prevent enemy planes landing troops on the flat broad Mendip plateau. The track leads straight towards the trig point at Beacon Batch, the highest point on the Mendips.

Hitherto, distant views on this walk have been mainly to the north and west, but here the scene opens to the south, with Brent Knoll rising out of the Somerset levels, the Quantocks beyond and on a clear day even the heights of Exmoor. Westwards, you should be able to pick out the islands of Steep Holm and Flat Holm, and Cardiff beyond.

From the trig point take the track running due south. At first this is still on the level, over the flat top of Blackdown, but after a while the land begins to dip and soon the open heathland ends and cultivation begins. Turn right along a path running by the side of a hedge. After a short distance this path turns left to join a minor road. Walk right along the road for a few yards and then left along a stony farm track and public footpath to Piney Sleight Farm. Ignore footpath signs off to the left and right, keeping straight on through the farmyard over the stile and across the field behind the farm buildings. The path is barely visible here, but soon it climbs a small rounded hill. Over this, and the view opens out across the Somerset levels, with the almost circular Cheddar reservoir clearly visible in the foreground.

National Trust property commences here, and the last mile is a magnificent descent into Cheddar, through rough woodland with the towering cliffs of Cheddar Gorge away to the left. The path is way-marked, which is necessary, as innumerable small tracks criss-cross through these woods.

Cheddar itself is of course famous for its caves. These have made the little town one of Somerset's major tourist centres, but the caves, with their multicoloured stalactites and stalagmites, have a beauty of their own which still manages to transcend the air of commercialism about Cheddar. There are other attractions in Cheddar, such as a museum, aquarium and numerous inns and cafes before your return to Bristol is made by bus No. 370, approximately every two hours.

Alternative Route

A somewhat shorter walk, perhaps more suitable for a winter's day when dusk comes early, can be made by starting from Shipham village instead of Churchill Gate. Take bus No. 369 to Shipham Turnpike, and on alighting turn back up the lane through the village.

In the eighteenth century Shipham was a savage and uncontrollable

Cheddar Gorge

village inhabited by lead miners. The writer and social reformer Hannah More wrote that 'no constable dares arrest a Shipham man for fear he should himself be waylaid, murdered and concealed in one of the many mining pits around the village, for this method of dealing with zealous officers has been employed many times.'

There is nothing of this savagery now in the neat dormitory of modern detached houses that Shipham has become. The modern residents are excellent gardeners and at most times of the year the gardens are a blaze of colour.

The made-up road ends abruptly at the end of the village and a bridleway leads straight into the wood. After a hundred yards or so, take a narrow track down to cross a stream with a Waterworks Company's hut on your right. After wet weather this path can be very muddy. The track runs up to the left and then keeps straight on through the wood. It is wide at this stage and much used by horses. Ignore cross paths and keep straight on. At a junction, take the left forking track. Continue along this for half a mile or so of quite delightful woodland. The path emerges onto the open heathland of Blackdown. Keep straight on, and the path leads up to the trig point at Beacon Batch. Indeed the last few hundred yards up to the Beacon is over the same track as that taken by the main route. From Beacon Batch, the descent into Cheddar is as described above.

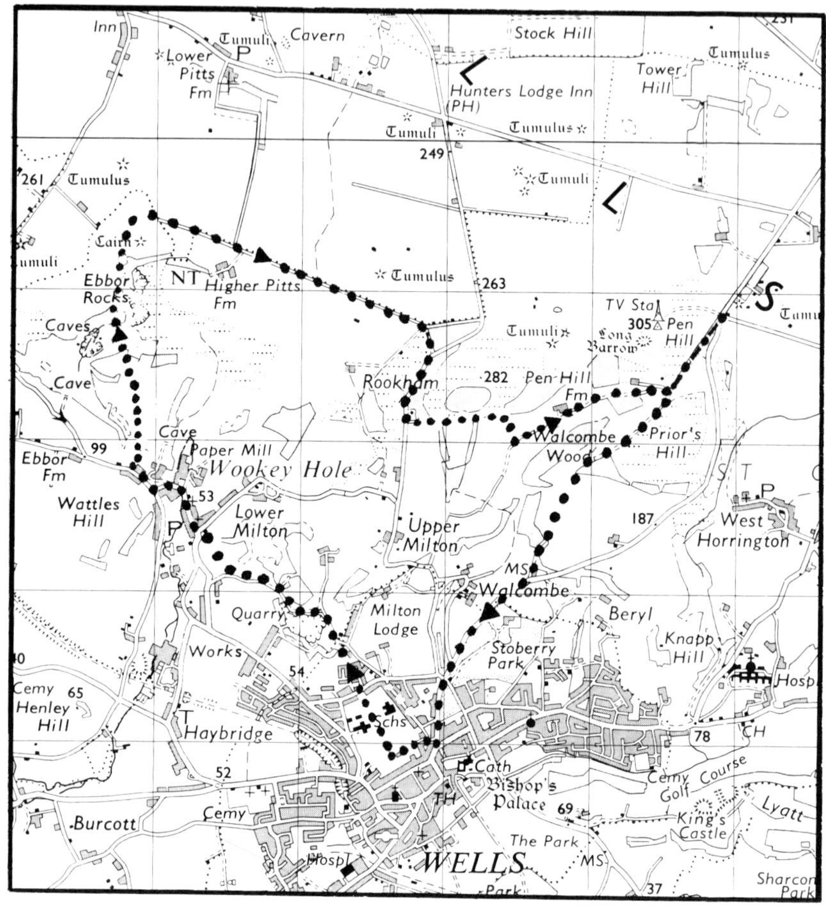

O.S. 182   •–•–• shorter walk

5 A SOUTHERN MENDIPS WALK FROM WELLS (8 miles)

Kenneth Pinnock

*Travel: Bristol Bus No. 376 from Bristol to Wells. Return by same
method from Wells, or from the bus stop near the TV Station, as
mentioned below (G.R. 569488). Motorists: Ample car parking in
Wells.*
*Refreshments: Cafes and pubs in Wells and in the vicinity of Wookey
Hole. Otherwise take packed food.*
[Map: Ordnance Survey 1:50,000 Series, Sheet 182.]

This ramble takes us past the famous caves at Wookey Hole and through
the Ebbor Gorge National Nature Reserve. Easy country tracks return
us to Wells, or the walk can be shortened by catching the bus back to
Bristol from the main A39 road near the entrance to the Pen Hill
Television Station.

From the junction of the Bristol (A39) and the Shepton Mallet
(A371) roads on the outskirts of Wells walk a few yards towards
Bristol and then turn left at a pillar box into a lane. Turn right at the
top, then almost immediately left, continuing on a right-hand path
between hedges, with a playing field on your right. Take the obvious
path on the right, from almost opposite the end of a stone wall
(G.R. 546449), past the Blue School buildings, through a swing gate
and so alongside the left hedge to a crossing road in a housing estate. (If
you have your camera with you, you can get a very good long shot of
the cathedral from this path. Behind you, to your right is a distant view
of Glastonbury Tor, standing conspicuously above the vast surrounding
moorland.)

Cross the road, and continue along a signposted footpath, climbing
steadily and crossing a second road and so up to the field at the top, via
a stile at G.R. 543466. Continue ahead to the right of a fenced-in
quarry, and turn left at the end of it along a minor road for about a
quarter of a mile (G.R. 537471), where you will find a wooden stile and
hand-gate set in the hedge on the right, opposite two iron field gates.
Follow the grassy path through the field, starting almost parallel with
the road, and arrive at a hand-gate in the bottom right corner. Continue
alongside the left hedge in the next field, soon passing through a gap to
another hand-gate into a third field. Still following the left hedge, join
the road at G.R. 533474 via a gate opposite a rank of houses. Go along

the road right, past the Wookey Hole Caves complex soon to bear right at the fork along the Easton/Cheddar road. Now look for a cottage on the right called 'Elm Batch'. Go through the hand-gate here, and follow a clear path into a field. Ignore the left (lower) track inside, but continue more or less straight ahead, through three more fields on a clear track, making for a set-back stile at a point a few yards left of a fence around the jutting-out section of facing woodland (G.R. 528486). You are now inside the Ebbor Gorge National Nature Reserve. Follow the rising track through the wood, ignoring all side paths and crossing tracks, soon rising out of the dip on the rocky path ahead up to a stile on the edge of woodland at G.R. 527489. Climb a wide stile in the fence immediately right, then cut across some rough grassland to a gap roughly in the middle of a low broken wall, a little to the right of a group of hawthorn trees. Cross the next field in the same direction, making for an obvious crossing of the wall facing you on the far side, marked by long wooden bars, a type of wall stile still common on Mendip. Climb over into the next field, and divert slightly right to a field gate in the right hedge. Now alongside the left wall to reach a crossing cart

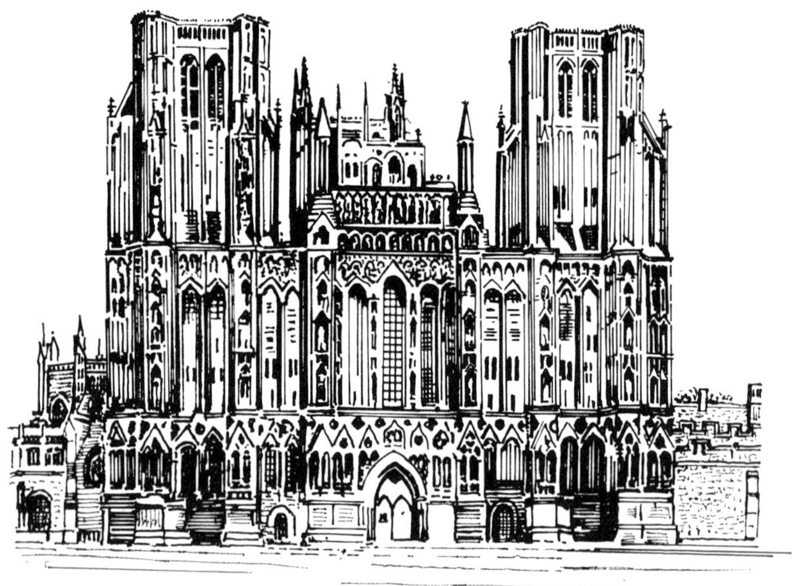

Wells Cathedral

track over a low wire fence (G.R. 528494), and follow this old Mendip
road to the right, past Higher Pitts Farm, after which the track becomes
a delightful green lane. In about a mile, at the abrupt left bend at
G.R. 549487, go through the gate on the right, and then go immediately
left alongside the fence. Soon descending over rough ground, make for a
gap between the end of a downhill-running fence and the wall at the
bottom. Join the road via the nearby gate, and follow it right to the
bridleway at the entrance to 'Ivy Cottage' (G.R. 547482). Follow the
track straight ahead through a gate bearing a 'Private Woodland' notice,
keeping strictly to the obvious path. Pass through a field gate at the
right corner and tip of some woodland (G.R. 554482). Now follow the
right edge of the next field (i.e. you will now have turned at right-angles)
to meet a clear crossing track at an open gateway (G.R. 554480). Here
turn left, soon passing Pen Hill Farm. Turn right shortly after, and right
again at a T-junction of tracks in a short distance (G.R. 566484), to
return you to Wells via a clear bridle track and later, the main road. Bus
users may prefer to turn left from the T-junction instead of right as
described above, to meet the main road in half a mile, where there is a
bus stop for Bristol near the gate to the Television Station.

Rectory Fm
Eastertown
North Yeo Fm
Hope Fm
Lympsham
Poplar Fm
Purving Row
Old River Axe
Lower Fm
Edingworth
Manor Fm
Wick Lane
Picnic Area
Rooks Bridge
Tarnock
Burton Row Fm
Slade Fm
Shrub Fm
East Brent
Chapel Fm
Brent Knoll
Lakehouse Fm
MP
Brent Ho.
Fort
137
Brent Knoll
Battleborough
M 5
Mark Yeo
White Cross
Inn
Vole Fm
Vole
Somerset Court
Chelsea Fm
Edithmead

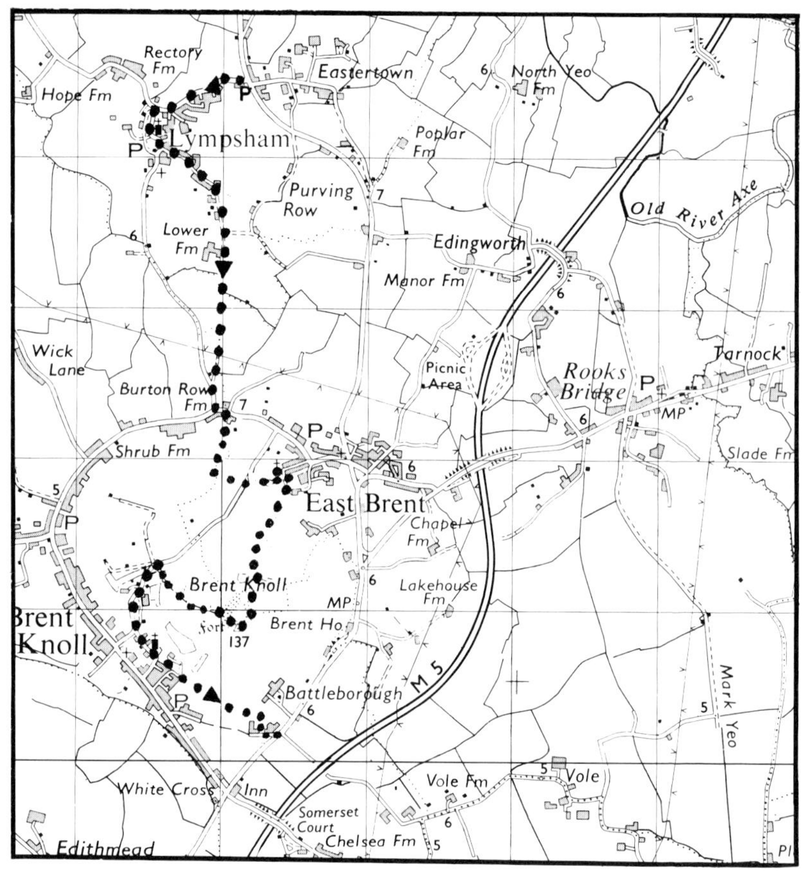

O.S. 182

6 LYMPSHAM AND BRENT KNOLL (4½ miles)

Kathleen Wiggins

*Travel: British Rail to Weston-super-Mare, then Bristol Bus Nos. 138 to
141 (inclusive) from Weston-super-Mare to Lympsham, Copse Corner.
Return by the same bus services from Battleborough Lane end.
Motorists: Lay-by on western side of A370 just past turning to
Lympsham, or limited parking in Lympsham village.
Refreshments: Knoll Inn, East Brent.
[Map: Ordnance Survey 1:50,000 Series, Sheet 182.]*

Brent Knoll is a solitary hill rising sharply from the low-lying pasture
land between Weston-super-Mare and Highbridge. Its distinctive shape,
with earthworks round the summit, indicates that it was once a hill fort,
and it was to the shelter of these earthworks that the Saxons retreated
when the Danes attacked this area in the ninth century.

This walks begins from the bus-stop at Copse Corner, on the A370
(G.R. 342545), some four miles south of Weston-super-Mare, almost
opposite the lane turning off to the small village of Lympsham. Cross
the A370 with great care and proceed for about half a mile down the
lane to the village.

Opposite the Manor Hall turn left along Church Road past
Lympsham Church, with its fine fifteenth-century tower, and on your
right a curious manor house, with Tudor-style parapets. Immediately
past the Post Office and the old forge fork left down South Road. After
walking between houses on either side for a few hundred yards, you will
find the aspect gradually opening out, with excellent views of Brent
Knoll to the right and Crook Peak, at the end of the Mendips, to the
left, with the Loxton valley beneath it. If you walk quietly past the
rhyne (drainage channel) which soon appears to the left of the road,
you may well be rewarded by the sight of a heron.

A little further along South Road you will come to a gate straight
ahead, and another to the right marked 'Lower Farm'. Just to the left
of the former the road continues as a broad track which leads on
through a gate after about 150 yards. In wet weather this track is likely
to be muddy, but not impassable. Gradually it becomes narrower,
twisting a little between high hedges, and after about half a mile it joins
a lane. Here you should turn left along the lane until it joins the B3140.

Turn left briefly along the B3140, and then take a signposted path to the right, opposite an attractive old white farmhouse. This path leads straight up by the side of a modern bungalow, and a garden fence beyond, through a field gate, and then rises gently by the left-hand edge of the field, alongside a ditch. Passing the remains of an old gateway, the path, still ascending, continues between a high blackberry hedge on the left and a steeply sloping field to the right. Watch out for the many rabbits and their holes here.

Near the top of the field the path turns left, down a bank, over a wooden stile and crosses a ditch by a plank bridge. Beyond the bridge climb a short, steep bank, into a long, narrow field. Follow the path along the left-hand side of this field, climb the white stile at the end into a lane and turn left, watching out for traffic. After twenty yards or so, another white stile is reached, on the right. Here you should pause to admire the view of the lovely parish church of East Brent, with the Mendips in the background, and Brent Knoll on your right.

Cross the white stile and follow a footpath down towards the church, with a hedge on your right. Turn left at the hedge round the churchyard and follow it round until you reach a kissing gate into the churchyard, whence an asphalt path leads down on your left to the church. The church (late thirteenth and early fourteenth centuries) was the property of Glastonbury Abbey until the time of the Dissolution. Note the unusual lath and plaster ceiling (*circa* 1637) with an embossed

Brent Knoll

design representing the crown of thorns, and look for the pretty stained glass window commemorating a former vicar who was both a naturalist and a keen cricketer.

If by now you have a thirst, make a short detour down the road into East Brent village to the Knoll Inn, situated on the small triangle of minor roads on the other side of the A370.

Returning to the church, take the path along the lower edge of the churchyard by a wall, go through a kissing gate into a yard, where there are some temporary school classrooms, and straight across the yard to another kissing gate signposted 'Footpath to the Knoll'. From this gate take the clear path running diagonally across the field to a stile in the opposite corner, and continuing thence straight up towards the top of the Knoll to become the summit of a gently sloping ridge. Then after crossing two further stiles a short scramble up the steep-sided ramparts will bring you to the top.

As you stand there in the breeze notice the curious way in which the ramparts conceal a large hollowed-out area within, presumably where the Saxons brought their women, children and flocks to protect them from the Danish raiding parties. Then, if you are lucky enough to be there on a clear day, you can admire the spectacular views all around. On the landward side, from north to south, can be seen Bleadon Hill, Crook Peak and the Mendips, and Glastonbury Tor, and if it is really clear, the Poldens and the Quantocks as well. To seaward, the view includes Brean Down, Steep Holm and Flat Holm (the two island bird sanctuaries in the Bristol Channel), and Hinkley Point Atomic Power Station.

Half-way round the ramparts you will reach a triangulation pillar, and a stone marking the site of various celebratory bonfires. From this stone walk clockwise round the ramparts for a short distance until you reach a clear path heading steeply downhill towards a prominent group of light-green farm buildings, with woods immediately behind them. Taking this path descend quickly to a blackberry hedge, cross a stile, and continue straight down through a field towards a gate in a hedge opposite. After crossing the adjacent stile the path runs diagonally across the next field towards the farm buildings and leads into a farm lane through an iron gate by a water trough. The lane takes you past an old barn on the right, and after about 50 yards joins a minor road, along which you turn left. After descending through pleasant woods into Brent Knoll village, you eventually reach a fork where you turn left along a road signposted 'The Knoll via Church'.

St Michael's Church, a short distance along this road on your left, should certainly be visited. The south door and one column near the altar are all that remain of the original Norman church, but there are many other things of interest, including the magnificent carved bench-ends, depicting in parable form a medieval story of the Abbot of Glastonbury, and the grand seventeenth-century memorial to John Somerset and his two wives.

At the sharp right bend in the road just past the church turn left through a kissing gate marked with a public footpath sign, and, after about 15 yards turn right before a large blackberry bush to follow a narrow path past a large house on your left. Just past the house turn right down the field and go through an iron gate by a water trough into a road, turning right and then almost immediately left into another road (Coombe Side) with bungalows on either side and a public foot-path sign. Between the two end bungalows you will find an iron gate next to a stile, and another sign. Cross the stile, follow the path between two hedges, cross another stile and continue along the top of a field to two more stiles. After climbing over the last one, scramble up a little bank and you will find the path following a contour line round the hillside, with a hedge on your right and a tussocky field stretching steeply uphill on your left. Passing through a gap in the hedge, continue still on the same contour line, through another gap in a blackberry hedge; then, after about 20 yards bear diagonally downhill to the right towards a corrugated iron barn. At the bottom corner of the field, an iron gate leads into a farmyard, from which a second gate leads into a farm lane. This lane bears to the right, and joins a more substantial lane at the corner of the farmhouse garden, by three fine yew trees. Turn left along this lane, to join the main A38 road; at this junction you can on request get a bus back to Weston-super-Mare or to the Lympsham turn-off, if you have left your car there.

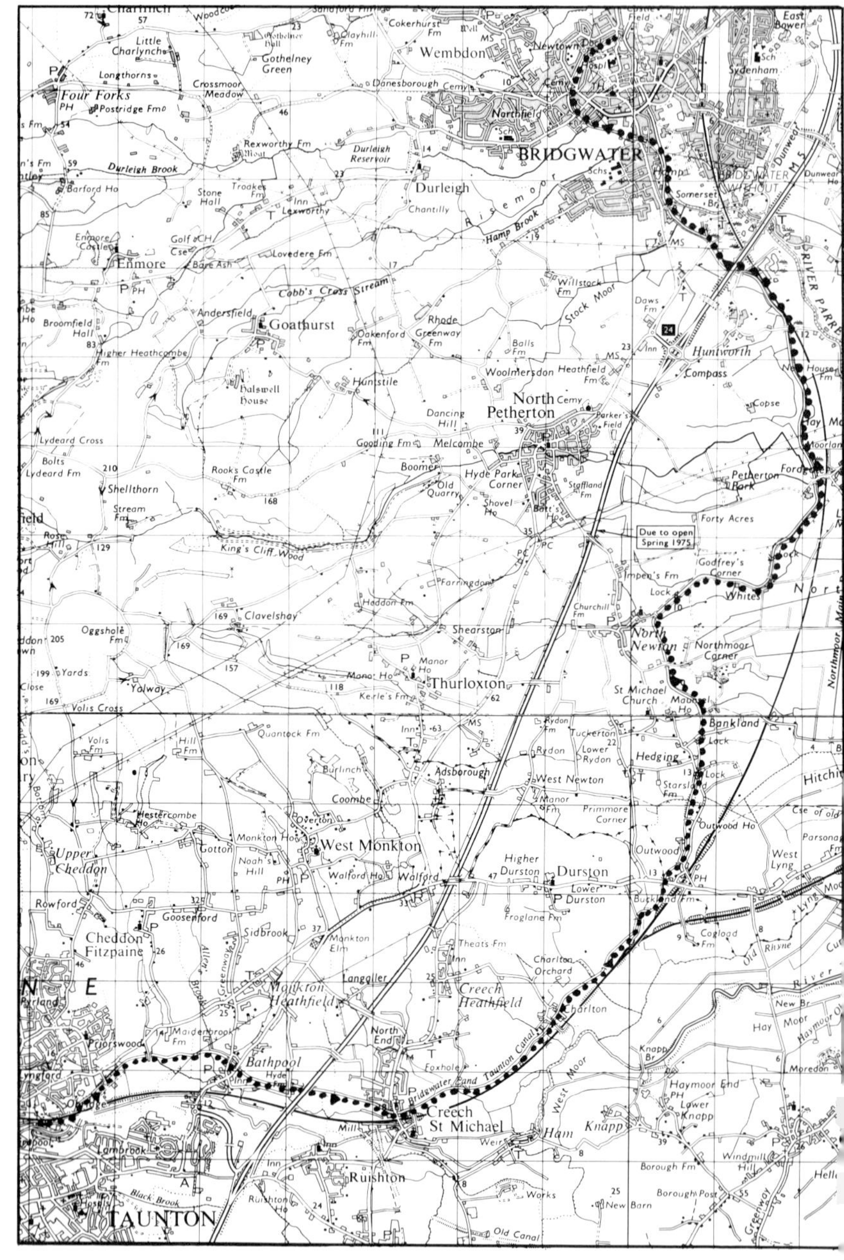

O.S. 182 and 193

7 THE BRIDGWATER AND TAUNTON CANAL (7½ miles, 10½ miles or 14½ miles)

Philip Daniell

Travel: British Rail to Bridgwater. Return either direct from Taunton by British Rail or via Western National Bus No. 266 (not Sundays) from Durston to Taunton or via Western National Bus No. 281 (not Sundays) from Creech St Michael to Taunton.
Refreshments: ample facilities in Bridgwater and Taunton; Boat and Anchor Inn, Huntworth Bridge; pubs at Durston and Creech St Michael.
[Map: Ordnance Survey 1:50,000 Series, Sheets 182 and 193.]

Cross-country arteries are not a new concept. Today we have the motorways, but about two hundred years ago a great system of trunk waterways was being developed, linking Thames, Severn, Mersey and Humber. Among the subsidiary waterway links so conceived was a ship canal from the Bristol Channel to the River Exe, to avoid the hazardous voyage round Land's End. Only parts of this ambitious project were ever completed, one of them the canal from Bridgwater to Taunton. As a highway this is now a nonsense; as a walk it's a delight.

Canals are not well served by public transport. Much of their charm is in their remoteness, so there are few 'escape routes' once you are launched along the tow-path of this one. However, you can reduce the total mileage of 14½ miles to more manageable proportions by leaving the tow-path at either Durston or Creech St Michael and catching a bus into Taunton, whence you can return to Bridgwater by train or bus. But be warned! Canals are addictive; always the next bend and the next lock beckon, and of course the miles are flat and easy. So when you get to either Durston or Creech you may well feel like walking right on to the terminus at Taunton.

The walk starts at Bridgwater Dock (G.R. 297376) which is about half a mile north of the town centre and adjacent to the western bank of the River Parrett, with which it was connected in its commercial heyday. So simply follow the path alongside the river on the western side until you come to the dock on your left. If you are on the eastern side of the river (e.g. at the Bus Station) you can cross the river by an old iron bridge at G.R. 300375. Useful landmarks adjacent to the dock are a factory chimney in decorative red and cream brickwork and a huge mound of earth, presumably from the original excavations for the dock.

Bridgwater Dock

I am fascinated by dead industrial landscapes. Bridgwater Dock is
dead, and it is magnificent. Observe the old warehouses, the former
Canal and Dock Office (still with its G.W.R. lettering), the blocked-off
locks, the wild flowers where once there was commerce. If you do not
share my fancy, be on your way, Taunton-bound.

The town and the traffic go about their affairs overhead. Soon you
are walking through a brick-lined cutting. After about 2 miles cross to
the east bank of the canal, and ahead is the great sweep of the new M5.
Despite the motorway, this is a rural scene, with cows and geese and a
delightful pub, not long re-opened — the Boat and Anchor. The pubs
were very much a part of the canals, often having stables for the horses
which drew the boats and being social centres for the canal people who
lived a life remote from the rest of the community. As the canals come
back to life, so do their pubs.

This is not meant to be an exciting walk. There are no great features
or sudden vistas. It is a flat and quiet agricultural landscape. If it were
just a footpath, it would be dull. But here there is always the water
alongside, with its special plant and bird life, the quickly glimpsed fish;
and all round you there is blissful, isolated peacefulness.

The canal meanders across the flat Somerset levels, passing tiny half-
forgotten hamlets, crossed occasionally by minor roads or farm tracks,

46

and punctuated at irregular intervals by locks which raise it gradually to the level of the River Tone at Taunton.

About a mile after passing the last of these locks the canal passes under a small accommodation bridge and enters a shallow cutting. Ahead is the Glastonbury Road Bridge carrying the A361 over the Canal. Just before this bridge, on your left, is the British Waterways Board's modest Durston maintenance yard. Obviously this is the moment to explain the status of this canal. Of the 2,000 miles of nationalised waterways, 300 are used for commerce and 1,100 for re-creation. The odd 600 miles are known, logically enough, as the Remainder. For these the Board is required by Statute to achieve the most economical solution for them. This could mean just filling them in, but the Board have chosen instead to work with local authorities to restore most of these Remainder Waterways for navigation and leisure. Here on the Bridgwater and Taunton, restoration is taking place, financed by the local council. It's a slow and evolutionary process, but one day small boats will again be able to navigate the whole length of the canal. Today, we can enjoy walking its towing path, or can canoe on some of its stretches.

If you now want to break off the walk (having done some 7½ miles) you can climb up the bank on the left to gain access to the A361 (watching out for fast traffic) and walk along the road eastwards for about 300 yards where you will find a bus stop. Here you can get a 266 bus into Taunton.

Three miles further along the tow-path brings you to Creech St Michael, the only settlement of any size along the canal, with two pubs and some not unattractive modern housing development, and here is another opportunity for you to end the walk and get a bus into Taunton.

If you decide at this point to continue the walk into Taunton, either there and then or on some later occasion, there are several features of interest to look out for. For instance, just beyond Creech is the site of the junction with the long-defunct Chard Canal. Although there is nothing of the actual junction now to be seen, about a third of a mile inland on the outskirts of the village are the remains of the great aque-duct which carried the Chard Canal to the junction. A little further on, at Bathpool, there are small boats for hire. The final stretch of tow-path leading into Taunton is not very impressive but there is a final treat before you make your way to the railway station. At Firepool Lock the canal ends, but beyond are the placid waters of the Tone and a fine weir down which its water tumbles. Where the railway warehouse now stands was once the junction with yet another canal, the Grand Western, intended to run to the River Exe, but eventuating only as a branch line to Tiverton. If this excursion has whetted your appetite for canal-walking, then I suggest a visit to Tiverton and a walk, or horse-drawn boat trip, along the Grand Western Canal which has been pleasantly restored.

I have tried not to overstate the attraction of the Bridgwater and Taunton Canal. I could show you better, but they are a long way from Bristol. This is a simple, modest walk — and it's all on the flat. If this is your first canalside walk, I must repeat my warning. There is something in the canal water which may grip and bewitch you. You may become another of those lost souls whose every weekend and holiday is devoted to walking yet more canals. You will not have time for the Costa Brava or Snowdon and your friends will be much less impressed when you tell them that you have seen Stourport, the Anderton Lift, or all Seven Wonders of the Waterways. But I know of no antidote to the dreaded canal bug; if you catch it, you may just as well enjoy it. I do!

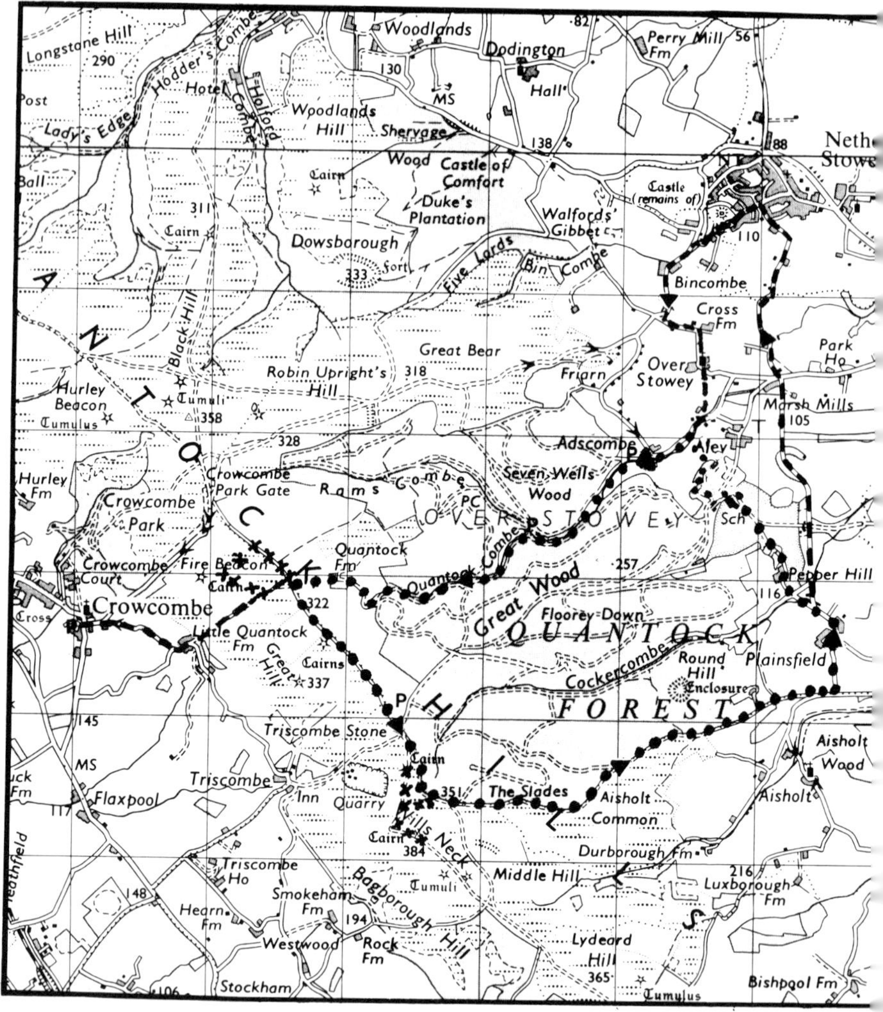

O.S. 181   xxxx diversion   – – – access routes

8 THE SOUTHERN QUANTOCKS (9½ miles via Nether Stowey; 8¾ miles via Crowcombe; 6¾ miles if you come by car).

Kate Ashbrook

Travel: British Rail to Bridgwater; thence by Western National Bus No. 215 to Nether Stowey (two-hourly service and not Sundays). Alternatively, British Rail to Taunton, thence by Western National Bus No. 218 to Crowcombe. Motorists: Car parks at Adscombe, Rams Combe, Crowcombe and Triscombe Stone.
Refreshments: Inns at Nether Stowey and Crowcombe.
[Map: Ordnance Survey 1:50,000 Series, Sheet 181.]

This walk includes a variety of Quantock scenery, passing through villages and deep wooded combes and out along the lovely Quantock ridge. It has been devised to make the best use of the limited public transport facilities in this part of Somerset, particularly for people coming from the Bristol area. It consists of a basic circular route through the heart of the Southern Quantocks (plus several optional diversions) which is ideal for people coming by car, plus extensions northwards, to give access to and from the bus service at Nether Stowey, and westwards, to give similar access for the bus service at Crowcombe. It will be seen from the map that various 'permutations' of the route are possible, e.g. a cross-Quantocks walk from Nether Stowey to Crowcombe. For convenience the route description begins from Nether Stowey.

Approaching Nether Stowey from Bridgwater one first sees the church which was, excluding the tower, rebuilt in 1851. Before entering it you will see on the left the grave of Thomas Poole, the philanthropist and friend of Coleridge. There is also a tablet to him on the south wall. Adjoining the church is the fifteenth-century manor house of Stowey Court, where cavaliers were garrisoned during the Civil War.

Entering the village you pass two inns and come to the clock tower by the bus-stop. If you fork right here you will reach the house where Coleridge lived from 1797 to 1800 and wrote 'The Ancient Mariner' and 'Khubla Khan', and which now belongs to the National Trust. It is open to visitors from April to September (2–6 p.m.) but not on Fridays and Saturdays. Castle Street, beside which a stream flows, is to the left of the clock tower, and contains the house where Tom Poole lived and had his tan-yard; a pathway led through this to Coleridge's house.

Proceed along Castle Street to Castle Hill. At the summit a footpath on the right leads to a prominent mound, the only remains of the Norman castle on much older earthworks, and destroyed to provide building materials for Stowey Court.

Continue along the road, turning left at the junction through Bincombe to Over Stowey. The ornate church here has beautiful carved bench-ends and a Burne-Jones window in the north transept wall. Just beyond the village follow the footpath from Glebe Cottage on the right, across two fields, rejoining the road to the left of a pink cottage, and, turning right, proceed to Adscombe, where there is a car park. You are now on the basic circular route.

Follow the sign pointing straight ahead to 'Quantock Forest Trail', passing the attractive Adscombe Farm and branching left at the fork. Spruce trees grow on the right, and on the left flows a stream bordered by deciduous trees. At the next car park, at Rams Combe, turn left, crossing the stream into Quantock Combe, and at the next fork bear right. In the summer this is a good place for butterflies, and you may even be lucky enough to see buzzards here. At the next fork turn right again and over a stile on the left. The track leads along the edge of the wood and soon the now unoccupied Quantock Farm appears. After crossing the lawn you pass the house and farm buildings, and proceed alongside a bank of beech trees, crossing two fields, and emerge via a gate at the top on to the old drove road running along the Quantock ridge, and thought originally to be Neolithic.

(At this point the access route from Crowcombe, climbing up the combe via Little Quantock Farm, joins the basic route, more or less in line with the path on which you have just travelled. If you wish to see something of this delightful village, and have the necessary time and energy, it is worth your diverting off the basic route here. The village is just over a mile away at the foot of the hills. En route you can also visit Fire Beacon Hill where a fire was lit when the Spanish Armada threatened invasion. There are marvellous views towards Exmoor from the top. Crowcombe's fifteenth-century church is noteworthy: the spire was struck by lightning in 1725 and the top piece now stands in the churchyard. Observe the medieval cross outside the south door, the fan vaulting in the porch, the carved pews and the graceful tower arch. The Church House stands opposite and nearby is Georgian Crowcombe Court (now a school). The village possesses several shops and an inn, and of course there is the bus service to Taunton.)

Turn left following the lovely drove road shaded by beech trees, with

Crowcombe Village

a spectacular view westwards, for three-quarters of a mile to the small wishing stone, the Triscombe Stone, where two tracks intersect. The name probably originates from 'trista' or meeting place, suggesting that lords and tenants, or hunts, used to meet here, as the Devon and Somerset Staghounds do now. It is worth making a short diversion to the great hill of Will's Neck ahead to your right; this is the highest point on the Quantocks, the name meaning 'ridge of the Britons', and there are Neolithic tumuli here. From the summit Bridgwater Bay, Wales, Exmoor, North Hill above Minehead, the Blackdowns, and, on a clear day, even Yes Tor on Dartmoor can be seen.

Continue along the drove road from Triscombe Stone, keeping to the edge of the forest with the open heath of Aisholt Common and a splendid view to the right. After 2¼ miles the track joins a road, and you take the next turning to the left to Plainsfield, where the old smithy is used to demonstrate weaving. In half a mile at the fork turn left for Pepper Hill, where the basic route forks left and the eastern arm of the Nether Stowey access route forks right.

To complete the circle to Adscombe or to return to Nether Stowey

by a longer but more attractive route (the direct access route following
the road through Marsh Mills with its old aqueduct), follow the track
left past the buildings of Pepper Hill Farm and the wood and then
through Quantock Park with its tall, assorted trees. On the left is an
imposing Victorian school, the track bearing left past the new buildings.
Now turn down to the right, passing an unusual house with a belfry
containing dovecotes. Before reaching a small car park, turn left down
through a wood to the road, this being an old entrance to Quantock
Park. Turn left at the road for Adscombe (and right for Nether Stowey,
so retracing your steps through Over Stowey), noting in the first field
on the left the trees marking the site of the now ruined Adscombe
Chapel, founded in the tenth century by the monks of Athelney Abbey.
A short walk brings you to Adscombe.

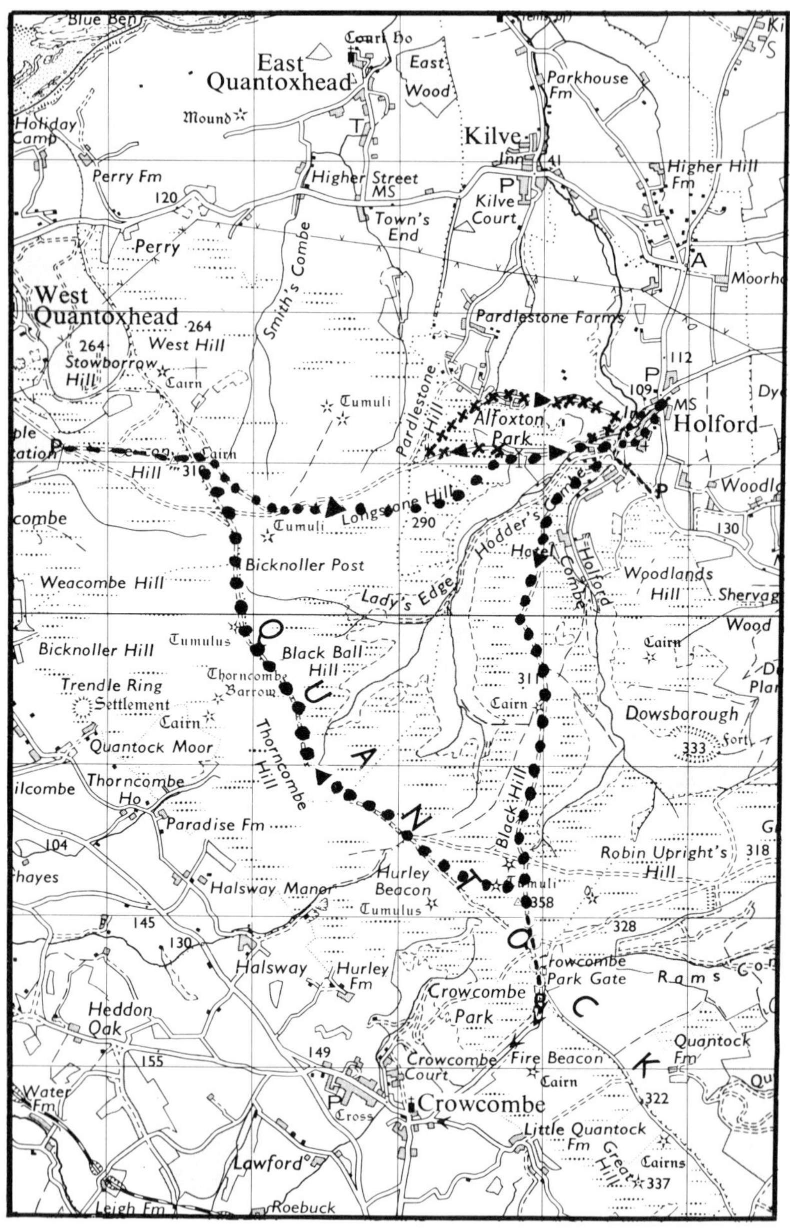

O.S. 181   ×××× diversion   — — — access routes

9 THE NORTHERN QUANTOCKS (6 miles)

Stephen Taylor

*Travel: British Rail to Bridgwater, then Western National Bus No. 215
(not Sundays) from Bridgwater Bus Station to Holford, Plough Inn.
Alternatively, British Rail to Taunton, then Western National Bus
No. 218 to Crowcombe, and walk north-eastwards thence up road to
join route near Crowcombe Park Gate. Motorists: Park in lay-by on
A39, quarter of a mile south of Holford, or at Crowcombe Park Gate,
or near Staple Plantation, West Quantoxhead.
[Map: Ordnance Survey 1:50,000 Series, Sheet 181.]*

If you have never visited the Quantock Hills this walk will whet your
appetite for seeing much more of this compact, delectable Area of
Outstanding Natural Beauty, as it is officially designated. The views
from the hilltops are magnificent, the many paths and tracks are clear
and firm, and if you can avoid the busiest times of the holiday season,
you will find blissful peace and solitude. No wonder two of our
greatest poets, Wordsworth and Coleridge, loved and were inspired by
these hills and chose to live for a while at their feet.

The main mass of the Quantocks forms an almost continuous ridge
running south-eastwards from West Quantoxhead. On its seaward side
this mass is broken up by delightful deep wooded combes, each with its
stream. This walk, however, keeps mainly to the tops of the hills, to
give you almost a bird's eye view of the area. This invigorating, high,
open moorland offers little shelter, of course, so the walk is best not
undertaken in bad weather.

From the Holford bus stop on the A39 take the principal road into
the village passing plain little St Mary's Church on your left. At the T-
junction turn left and at the next junction turn right to reach a pleasant
village green with a seat set in the centre. (Those coming by car can
reach this green by walking along the side road at the back of the A39
lay-by, ignoring the sign to Holford Combe, but following the sign to
Alfoxton and Hodder's Combe.) Almost facing the seat is a cottage, to
the left of which is a track curving uphill (G.R. 155411). Follow this
track as it rises steadily south-westwards above the village. Below you
on your right is Hodder's Combe, whilst on your left is Holford Combe
with the large water-wheel set in the centre of Combe House (now a
hotel). Keep on this firm, stony track as it curves gently leftwards and

climbs up and up past Dowsborough (or Daneborough) Hill (333 metres; 1093 ft.) crowned with its Iron Age fort away on your left and a cairn off to your right. The main Quantock ridge now looms up ahead.

In this deserted area of gorse, heather and bracken you may be lucky to encounter a small group or two of wild ponies. There are red deer here too, but they are more likely to be seen in the shelter of the combes. This is ideal country for horse and pony riding, so you will doubtless meet the occasional rider in the course of your walk, or even a string of pony-trekkers. (Incidentally, there are many sheep roaming at will on the hills, so if you bring a dog please keep it firmly in control.)

After crossing another track at right angles climb to the top of the ridge and the triangulation column on Black Hill (358 metres; 1175 ft.), pausing to admire the views, particularly those south-westwards towards the Brendon Hills. Now you can pick up the main track which runs the entire length of the Quantocks and follow it north-westwards, keeping to the hilltops all the way. Look out for prehistoric tumuli from time to time on either side. Eventually near Bicknoller Post you have Beacon Hill (310 metres; 1017 ft.) with its triangulation column directly ahead

The Quantocks from Willett Hill

of you. Choose the track which takes you over the right-hand shoulder of the hill and then take the short spur leftwards from this track to reach the summit, where on a clear day you can get superb views over Somerset and across Bridgwater Bay to Wales. In early June the lower slopes towards West Quantoxhead are enlivened by masses of rhododendrons in bloom.

Now retrace your steps to the main track and cross straight over it to a clear path going directly ahead which eventually links up with a larger track running along the seaward side of the hills and giving lovely coastal views. Ignore any left turns but keep straight on at a high level. At last at Longstone Hill you begin to descend towards Holford. With Hinkley Point power station ahead of you in the distance aim for a small clump of conifers which you pass on your right. These were planted to commemorate local people who served in the last war. (Look out for the little inscribed stone.) Ahead below you is a long belt of trees, including many venerable windswept beeches, running at an angle to your path. Turn right when you get to them and descend by a stony track soon enclosed by trees, which emerges on to a tarmac road leading to the village green. You can now return to the main road by taking the narrow lane (left fork), which runs alongside the stream to come out conveniently by the Plough Inn.

For those with some surplus energy the last part of the walk can be varied by turning *left* at the belt of trees and then turning half-right at the last large beech, to enter the corner of the wood by a clear path. This descends through the wood and eventually goes through a gate to become a tarmac road, through the gracious grounds of Alfoxton Park. The big white house on your right, now a hotel, was once the home of William Wordsworth. Keep on this road until it reaches the village.

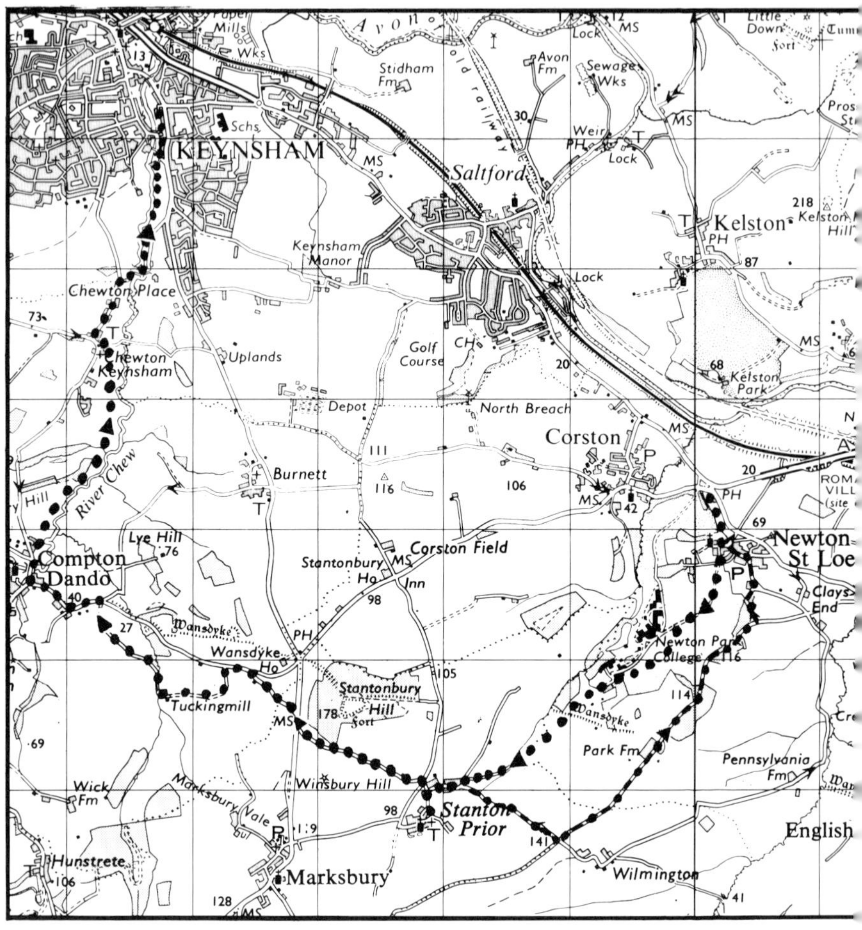

O.S. 172   •—•—• shorter walk

10 NEWTON PARK AND STANTONBURY (5½ miles or 9 miles)

Harold Overton

Travel: Bristol Bus No. 339 from Bristol or Bath to Globe Inn, Newton St Loe. Motorists: Park near Globe Inn at junction of A4, A39 and B3110 (traffic lights), or drive up hill to Newton St Loe village and park there.
Refreshments: Globe Inn, Newton St Loe; Gamekeeper Inn, Compton Dando.
[Map: Ordnance Survey 1:50,000 Series, Sheet 172.]

This walk takes you through pleasant wooded parkland enclosing a Georgian mansion and remains of a medieval castle with reputed associations with King John, and visits two interesting old churches. If you wish, you can extend it westwards around Stantonbury Camp (Iron Age) and through Compton Dando,whose medieval church has a Roman altar-stone built into its outer wall.

The walk starts on a field-path just to the left of the Globe Inn car park (G.R. 701653), going up the hill in a clear line to Newton St Loe village, whose name derives from William the Conqueror's having allotted the manor to one of his followers from St Lo in Normandy. Note the ancient 24-hour 'scratch dial' on the outside of the handsome church; it is not clear what did duty for the sun at night! The railing surrounding the eighteenth-century tomb of Joseph Langton in the churchyard is remarkable for the earliest use of cast iron in Somerset.

From the church retrace your steps to a short road leading to the gates of Newton Park. The public right of way is along the drive for about half a mile, until about 20 yards from another gate and a house resembling a second lodge. The path now forks to the left of the drive over a field (ploughed in winter), passing through a gate behind the house. Continue through fields, keeping parallel to the drive. Looking across the drive you see the Georgian mansion of the one-time Earl Temple, now flanked by the modern buildings of Newton Park College. A little further on there is a glimpse of the castle keep (*circa* 1400) where King John (died 1216!) was reputed to have been held captive by a rebellious baron.

The path continues between a little wood and the rear of a long farm building, emerging into playing fields. Keep on in the same general

Newton St Loe Village

direction and you will reach a green lane ('Washpool Lane'), leading directly into Stanton Prior at a road T-junction. This tiny village owes its name firstly to an old stone quarry ('Stone-Town'), and secondly to its having housed a priory under the rule of Bath Abbey. Little of the priory can now be seen, apart from the thirteenth-century church — left from the T-junction — whose most interesting feature is the grisly memorial (*circa* 1650) to one Thomas Cox.

Choice A — 5½ miles

Having inspected the village, return almost to the point where Washpool Lane met the asphalt roads. Here turn right and go up the road, which leads to Wilmington. In about three-quarters of a mile you will come to cross-roads, where turn left along a lane commanding extensive views over Newton Park and beyond, with Stantonbury Hill prominent to the left. After a wooded stretch, a left-hand turn takes you sharply down-hill into Newton St Loe, and so back to the Globe Inn by road, or the original field-path if preferred.

Choice B – 9 miles

From Stanton Prior, head along the road towards the wooded hill seen to the north-west. Passing Poplar Farm on your right, and ignoring a left turn, you come to a fork in the road. At this point a footpath yielding marvellous views should lead to the top of the hill, known locally as Stantonbury Camp, which is in fact an Iron Age fort, later incorporated in the Wansdyke, the great earthwork boundary of Wessex running from Thames to Severn. At the time of writing this path is impracticable following extensive tree-felling and replanting, but negotiations for its restoration are proceeding, and it will be worth checking to see if a public footpath sign has yet appeared as a result. Meanwhile take the lane on the left instead. After half a mile this strikes the main A39 Bath–Wells road. Turn right for a little way and then left down a minor road for quarter of a mile. Turn in left to a short rough lane which becomes a cart track through fields down to the tiny hamlet of Tuckingmill.

The hamlet is now nothing more than a farm and a couple of cottages, but cross the stream by the footbridge and you will see an enclosure surrounded by a low ruined wall. This is the site of one of the earliest Nonconformist chapels and its burying-ground, dating from the Five Mile Act of 1665 which forbade dissenting clergy to hold meetings within 5 miles of a corporate town.

Having crossed the footbridge, turn right on to a narrow causeway alongside the stream, which here shares the same course as the lane. However, the stream soon goes its own way and, weather permitting, you can walk the lane dry-shod. In another half-mile turn left at the cross-roads into the village of Compton Dando with its notable church and the Gamekeeper Inn.

In Compton Dando, cross the River Chew by the stone bridge and immediately enter the field on the right. Keep on the left side of this field to climb over a stile, up a short steepish bank, then close to the hedge on the right of the next field (subject to ploughing and growing crops). In the next field again, keep fairly close to the right-hand post and rail fence, past an iron gate, then through a wooden gate into a short stretch of green lane, which may get a little overgrown in summer, but it is still passable. Emerging from this woody stretch, the path bears almost due north, first slightly uphill to a stile, then slightly downhill by way of two stiles and an iron gate to reach a lane. Here turn up left into Chewton Keynsham, then right on the road leading to

Keynsham.

After half a mile this road zig-zags to cross the River Chew (note the old millpool and attractive gardens). Where the road straightens out again an iron post marks the start of a riverside field-path into Keynsham. Turn up right where this path meets a lane, then left along the road ('Wellsway') until it meets the Bath Road, with its bus-stops for Bristol, and (across the road by the Talbot Hotel) for Bath (or the Globe Inn if you have left your car there).

Lydes Fm
165
118
Buckland
Dinham
75
Murtry
Hill
119
The
160
Murtry
Hill
Barrow Hill
86
Fm
MS
Brookover
145 Newbury
Hill
67
Fm
Mill
Spring Gardens
sh Ponds
E L M
90
P
Bedlam
Hapsford
Weir
115
P
Great
Elm
Vale
Mells
P
Wadbury
Vallis
Fm
Sewage
Works
fort
Tedbury
Camp
MS
118
Cemy
95
125
le Green
Egford
Murder
Combe
134
Whatley Bottom
FROME
103
Gibbet Hill
137
Whatley
Hospl
Critchill
Fm
The Butts
Lower
Whatley
ROMAN VILLA
(site of)
ry
Southfield
Ho
112
Nunney Brook
Marston
Gate
114
Key
e
orner
120
Sharpshaw
Fm
S
Blat
Castle
Springfield Ho
Little
Sharpshaw Fm
Nunney
P
Berry
Hill
Marston Ho
Manor
Fm
Tytheri
The
Combe
135
Cheese Hill
MS

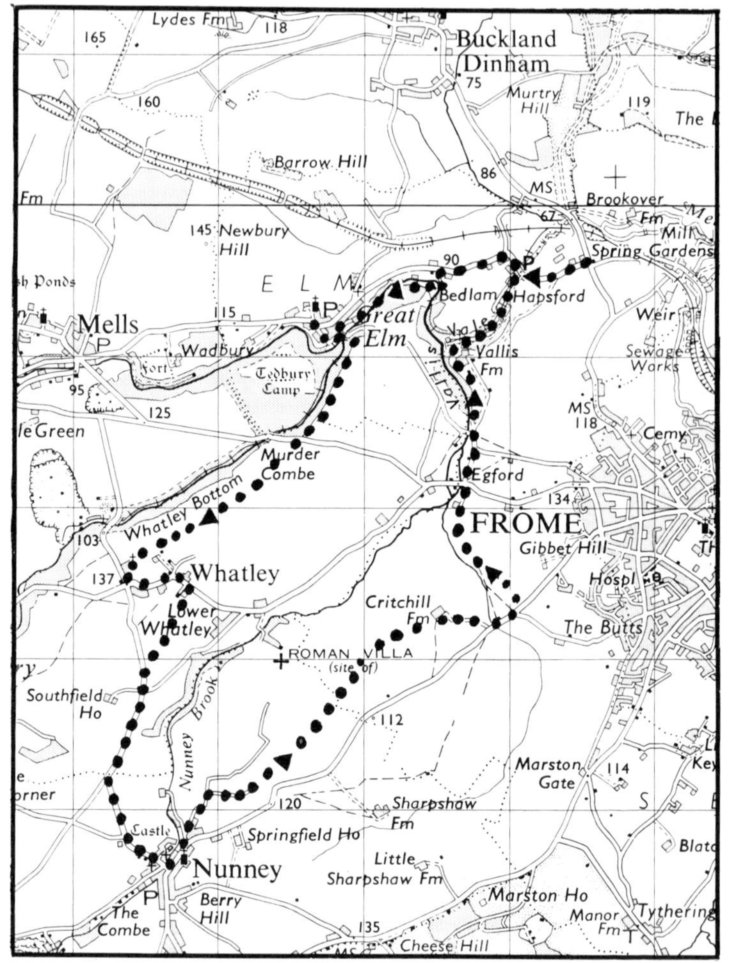

O.S. 183

11 GREAT ELM, MURDER COMBE AND NUNNEY (8½ miles)

Bill Parfitt

Travel: From Bristol take Bristol Bus No. 367 (Bristol–Frome) to Spring Gardens which is about 1½ miles north of Frome on the A362 (G.R. 765496). Very restricted service on Sundays. From Bath take Bristol Bus No. 184 (infrequent on Sundays) to Great Elm and pick up route from there. Motorists: Use lay-by at Hapsford Bridge, about half a mile west of Spring Gardens on road to Great Elm (G.R. 761495). Refreshments: Swan Inn, Whatley; George Inn, Nunney.
[Map: Ordnance Survey 1:50,000 Series, Sheet 183.]

This walk takes you through the peaceful, lush countryside just to the north-west of Frome in Somerset and introduces you to a quite unexpected and very striking ruined castle.

Get off the bus at Spring Gardens, walk a few steps in the direction of Frome and then turn right along the minor road signposted to Great Elm, passing the lay-by at Hapsford Bridge, where motorists begin the walk. About half a mile from the bridge turn left down a track to Bedlam, a wooded area in which only one house now remains. (Incidentally, Bedlam is a corruption of Bethlehem and means any place that is out of the way or difficult to find.) Cross the stream by the footbridge and turn right on to a path alongside the single-line mineral railway which links Whatley Quarries with Frome.

In about half a mile the path brings you to the picturesque village of Great Elm with its lake. Climb up the hill to the church, which is worth visiting to see the Saxon stones and Norman herringbone masonry in the tower. The doorway is Norman and there is a tiny early lancet window above with five lights. The interior of the church is charming, with low Jacobean box-pews and an Elizabethan gallery reached by outside steps and resting on oak pillars.

Now retrace your steps to the lake; just opposite it find a path ascending through the woods of Murder Combe. The origin of this gruesome name is not known; certainly it was already in use in 974 AD when Athelstan gave the area to the monks of Glastonbury, so one can only speculate as to what awful atrocity took place here in the dim past. Follow the path for about a quarter of a mile along to the top left-hand corner of the woods and come out into the Mells–Frome

road. Turn left along the road for about 100 yards and then right
through a gateway on to a path which follows alongside the hedge
through three fields, with the spire of Whatley Church immediately
ahead of you. The path leads you out on to a road to the left of the
church near a cottage. Turn left along the road for a quarter of a mile
as far as the Swan Inn, where you will find an iron stile next to a bungalow. Climb the stile and go straight across three fields by path to join
the road for Nunney. At several points along this last section look out
for the Westbury White Horse on the distant hills to your left. Turn left
along the road and so come into Nunney.

This beautiful village is like a bit of medieval England, clustered as it
is around its fine fourteenth-century castle and moat and its fifteenth-
century church. The lively Nunney Brook, crossed by ancient bridges,
adds further interest to the scene, whilst the George Inn is an admirable
source of refreshments. Nunney Castle is now in the care of the Department of the Environment; a notice by the entrance gate tells you how

Nunney Castle

to obtain a key to gain admission. The four round towers are still in
fairly good condition, but the rest of the building is just a shell, the
breaches made by Parliamentary cannon in the Civil War (1640-45)
being clearly visible. The castle was built, to a French design, from 1373
onwards by John de la Mare, Sheriff of Somerset, who was given a
licence to 'fortify and crenellate his manse at Nunney'. The marks of
five floors can be traced on the walls and the fireplace and oven can
still be seen. In 1645 Colonel Fairfax came to attack and besiege the
castle, then held by Colonel Prater for the King. The stores of the 14
defenders began to run very low, but they still included one sucking
pig. This unfortunate creature was taken to the top of one of the
towers each day and its squealing caused the besiegers to believe that
a fresh pig was being slaughtered every day and that the castle was well
provisioned. However a deserter from the castle informed Fairfax of the
true state of affairs and surrender was not long in coming after that. In
the church you will find stone figures of the proud de la Mare families,
with Sir John himself lying on a window-sill.

Just past the village pond, now a bird sanctuary, with stone seats for
visitors, and near the Manor House, take a path to the left bordered by
a stone wall, and then turn right almost immediately afterwards across
the meadows, with Springfield Farm on your right. Continue straight
ahead along a green lane or 'drang way', arriving in about a mile at
Critchell Farm. Here turn right along a stony lane to the road to Frome
(the houses and chimneys of which can be seen to the right). Turn left
along the road for about 300 yards and then near a lonely cottage turn
off left on to a field-path by the side of a stream. This takes you to
Egford where you cross straight over one road and join another one
going ahead towards Great Elm. In a quarter of a mile when this road
bears left, a notice board at a stile directs you on to the public footpath through Vallis Vale. Leave the road and take the path to the right
through the green valley and alongside the stream, passing some quarry
stone and gravel installations at one point. You will eventually come
out on to the road and the lay-by at Hapsford Bridge. If you came by
bus turn right here for the main road and the bus stop for Bristol.

P
P
P
Buckland
Dinham
75
Murtry
Hill
119
86
MS
67
Brookover
Fm
Mill
Spring Gardens
90
Bedlam
Hapsford
Great
Elm
Vallis
Vale
Vallis
Fm
Weir
Sewage
Works
MS
118
Cemy
Egford
134
FROME
Gibbet Hill
Hospl
Critchill
Fm
The Butts
Orchardleigh
Ho
Weirs
Castle
83
The Down
Dairy
Bonnyleigh
Hill
99
54
Oldford
T
MP
Weir
Mell
Oldford Hill
Ho
83
99
School
Innox
Hill
74
Fromefield
Clink
74
TH
Keyford
Mills
Rodden
Manor
91
Southfield Fm

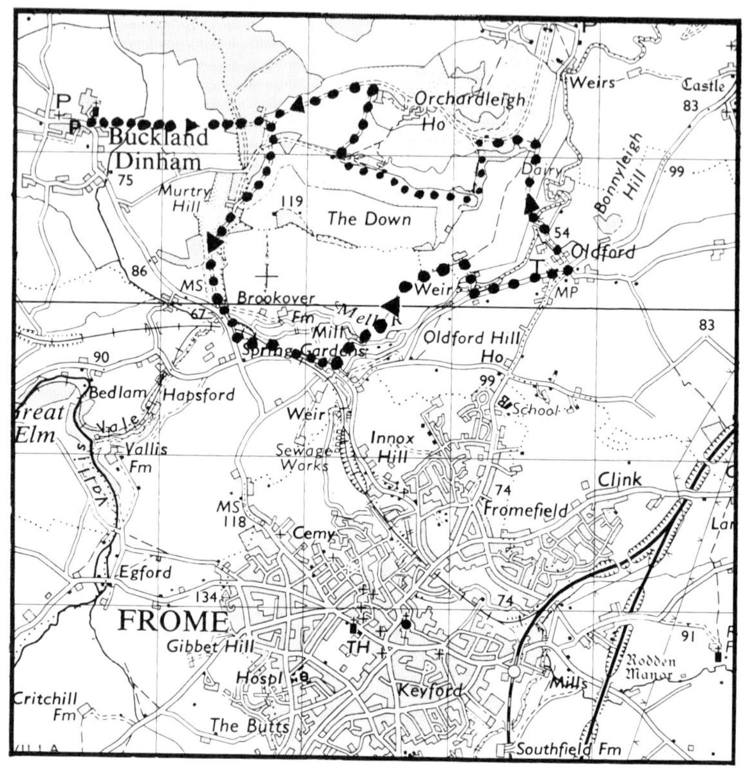

O.S. 183

12 BUCKLAND DINHAM AND ORCHARDLEIGH (9 miles)

Bill Parfitt

*Travel: From Bristol take Bristol Bus No. 367 (Bristol–Frome) to
Buckland Dinham Church. From Bath take Bristol Bus No. 253
(infrequent on Sundays) or No. 254 (not Sundays) to Oldford and pick
up route from there. Motorists: Park near the Church or elsewhere in
village.*
Refreshments: Ship Inn, Oldford.
[Map: Ordnance Survey 1:50,000 Series. Sheet 183.]

This walk takes you through some gracious Somerset parkland to see a
delightful old church surrounded on three sides by water.

Dismount from the bus at Buckland Dinham (G.R. 755512) and
first have a look round the church with its fifteenth-century tower and
Norman font. Sir John Denham and his lady lie in stone in their
chantry and have been here for six hundred years. Now climb over the
adjacent stile marked by a public footpath sign and take the path
through an orchard down to another stile and a footbridge. Cross both
these and, soon after, another footbridge, and then after going diagonally
up over a field (Murtry Down) climb over yet another stile. (If a crop is
growing in this field keep to the left-hand hedge.) If you look back now
you will see what a charming picture is made by the church and the
farm on the hill.

Now go through the gate opposite you and, keeping to the left-hand
hedge, cross a further stile at a wood. You are now entering the
Orchardleigh Estate with its abundance of game, particularly pheasants,
so please keep strictly to the footpath. Go straight through the wood,
past oak, ash, hazel, pine and horse chestnut, with pheasant coops and
pens on your left. At a new wooden stile in a quarter of a mile turn
right on to a tarmac path and follow it past two estate houses, looking
out for a glimpse of Orchardleigh Lake on the left through the trees.
The path winds to the left past a house dated 1867 and over a cattle
grid with the wood on the right and a notice board stating, 'Not to be
used by lorries or heavy traffic'. You are now passing through lovely
parkland. Note the charming estate cottage on the right with its
Orchardleigh arms. The estate path comes out on to the main road to
Frome via a pair of gate-houses with the Latin motto carved on the
eaves: *Pro patria non timidus mori auxilium meum Domino est* ('I am
not afraid to die for my country; my help is in the Lord'), whilst the

Orchardleigh House

stern warning on the board by the park gates says, 'No traffic allowed over private road. Visitors on foot admitted provided they keep to the footpaths. Dogs only on a lead.'

Turn left along the road for about 200 yards, over the old Bristol—Frome railway and the Mells River, until you come to an iron stile on the left. Climb over this into a field and follow the left-hand hedge to an opening by the ash tree in the corner and come out on to another road. (At the time of writing there is unfortunately some barbed wire across this opening.) Turn left along the road under the railway bridge into the hamlet of Spring Gardens, and at the cross-roads turn left to reach a timber yard in a quarter of a mile. Now cross the Mells River by bridge with a house on the left and a field-gate on the right. Go through the gate and follow the path across three fields to a farm, with the remains of an old coal canal near the left hedge. At the farm, turn right down to Mill House and the road to Oldford. Turn left along the road, and in about a third of a mile arrive at this village with refreshments available at the Ship Inn.

From the inn take the road signposted Lullington and again cross over the Mells River. In about half a mile, just past the large dairy

72

factory with its tall chimney across the fields on your right, find a stile
on your left. Climb over it and enter another fine area of Orchardleigh
parkland sloping uphill from the road and containing many fine trees.
Go half-right across this to meet a metalled drive coming in from your
right and follow this track leftwards until it reaches a charming gate
cottage. Here turn left down to Orchardleigh Lake and climb over a
stile near a romantic boat-house to reach the path running all along the
southern side of the lake. A notice here decrees, 'No bathing in the
Lake. No bicycles on paths. No damage to trees. No litter or fires.' The
lake contains many varieties of water-fowl, and at several points along
the path you will get fine views of Orchardleigh House set above a great
grassy slope and framed by trees. The house was built by Thomas Wyatt
in 1855 for the Duckworth family who still live there. Its predecessor
(a stone near the church marks the spot) was built for the Champneys
in the fifteenth century. The last of that line, who had no heir, was a
nineteenth-century gambler and spendthrift who died bankrupt, and the
land and the house then passed to Major Duckworth, who promptly
pulled the house down and had a new one erected in Elizabethan style.

At the western end of the lake on what is to all intents and purposes
a small island stands the unique little thirteenth-century Church of St
Mary. It has many medieval treasures, such as two stone monks on the
chancel walls with the hooks which once held the Lenten veil to screen
the altar, and an elegantly carved piscina and aumbry with its original
rough-hewn door and a small figure of Christ in a niche. Everywhere is
old stained glass, some with quaint saints, all beards and curly hair. Do
not miss the Norman font, with three of its panels completely finished
but the fourth one only just started. Visit the graves in the churchyard
of Sir Henry Newbolt (1862-1938), the noted patriot, poet and
educationalist, and his wife Mary (1867-1961). Inside the Church on a
beautifully carved stone is his epitaph:

Death is a gate and holds no room within
Pass — to the road beyond.

On leaving the church, turn right to follow a path leading up to another
gate-lodge and from here continue, right, towards Orchardleigh House.
This will give you a closer view of the mansion (which is very
occasionally opened to the public). At the house turn left and follow a
path through the parkland which in half a mile brings you to the same
stile you climbed to enter the estate on the outward journey. All you
need do now is to retrace your steps along the paths to Buckland

Dinham Church, which you can see ahead of you on the hillside three-
quarters of a mile away, and the bus for Bristol.

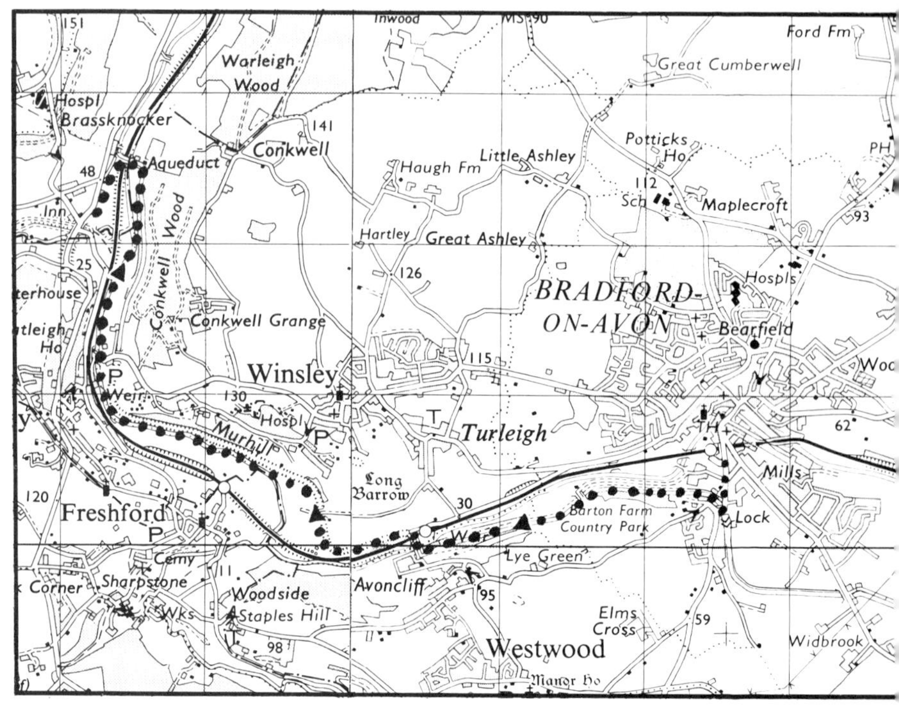

O.S. 172 and 173

13 THE KENNET AND AVON CANAL (4½ miles; longer walk 9 miles)

Ian Campbell

Travel: British Rail Bristol to Bradford-on-Avon. Hourly service weekdays. On Sundays use Bristol Bus No. 264 from Bath to Bradford. Return: Bristol Bus 264 Dundas Aqueduct to Bath, thence British Rail. Refreshments: Crossed Guns Inn, Avoncliff; Viaduct Hotel, north of Limpley Stoke.
[Map: Ordnance Survey 1:50,000 Series, Sheets 172 and 173.]

This walk goes through the deeply wooded Avon valley in Wiltshire, along the tow-path of the Kennet and Avon canal, now in process of restoration. The canal cuts right across southern England, and when fully restored will provide a through water route between London and Bristol, as it once did in its heyday. The waterway was opened in 1810, having taken some sixteen years to build. The engineer and architect was Rennie, and on this walk we shall see two of his best constructions, the aqueducts at Avoncliff and Limpley Stoke. Traffic was never as heavy as the promoters had hoped and the canal, suffering from competition with the Great Western Railway, declined steadily through the nineteenth century. In the 1930s the last regular traffic ceased and since the war sections of the canal have been dry. However, in the past few years tremendous progress has been made in restoration. Volunteers turn out at weekends to clear stretches, whilst the British Waterways Board works on the locks. The flight of locks up from Bath will soon be restored, making navigation possible through to the Dundas aqueduct.

To begin the walk, turn right from Bradford Station and after a couple of hundred yards the canal is reached. Turn right on to the tow-path at the Town Wharf. On the opposite bank a notice erected by the Canal Society calls for volunteers in the work of reclamation.

In the field to the right of the tow-path is the stone-built Great Tithe Barn, erected in the fourteenth century by the Abbess of Shaftesbury. The Cotswolds were sheep country and in the Middle Ages Bradford was a flourishing weaving centre. A substantial amount of tithe would have been collected in wool, and stored in this great structure by the Abbess and her successors. The Barn is open to the public on most days.

This is a delightful stretch of tow-path, with views northwards across

Tithe Barn, Bradford-on-Avon

the river Avon to Bradford clustered on its hill. The canal here has some
water, but is very shallow and will require a fair amount of dredging.
The opposite (south) bank is wooded, and even on a hot summer's day
there are the occasional stretches of shade across to the tow-path.

After about half a mile or so a swing bridge is reached and hereafter
the canal is without water for a few miles. For a couple of hundred
yards or so the bed is still damp, however, and this gives rise to a
botanist's delight of reeds and other waterside plants. The river Avon
itself comes close to the canal here, rushing quickly on its way thirty
feet or so below.

About a mile and a half from Bradford is the old weavers' hamlet of
Avoncliff. Here the canal takes a sharp right turn to cross the river Avon
on the aqueduct, built by Rennie in 1804. Pause half-way across and
look back the way you have come. The scene is one of the most delightful on the route, with the weir by the mill making a rushing water-

fall, the river running beneath and on the left the railway with minute
Avoncliff Halt, still open in 1976, the sort of country station all too
tragically passing into history. Another attraction of Avoncliff, if you
are here in opening hours, is the seventeenth-century gabled 'Crossed
Guns' by the south side of the aqueduct, set among the stone cottages
built for the weavers.

The canal and the tow-path take a sharp turn to the left and continue along the northern side of the valley now, hugging the 100-foot
contour with railway and river below on our left. The bed of the canal
is completely dry here and the reeds have given way to willowherb,
moon daisies and other limestone plants. The views are now all to the
south and west, whilst to the north the densely wooded hills rise
steeply up from the canal. Across the valley the occasional local train
stops at Freshford, another rural halt that mercifully survived the
Beeching axe of the sixties.

At the next village, Limpley Stoke, signs of the canal restorers can
be seen in the clearing of vegetation from the canal bed. New quarter-
mile posts proclaim the distance from Reading (where the canal joins
the Thames). After Limpley Stoke bridge the canal is again fully
watered, and the water is a picture with a plethora of water lilies. As the
canal becomes deeper and fresher, signs of water life can be seen — small
fish and the occasional swan.

About a mile from Limpley Stoke bridge, the canal takes a sharp turn
to the left to cross the river on Rennie's second construction on this
stretch of canal — the Dundas aqueduct. It is worth scrambling the 30
or so feet down to the riverside to see this magnificent structure from
below. So well does it blend with its surroundings that one is tempted
to think that Rennie built his aqueduct first and a sensitive river cut its
valley later.

On the far side of the aqueduct is a wharf and waiting place for
boats, and here our walk ends. Turn left up a steep slope to the main
road and a hundred yards or so back towards Bradford is the Viaduct
Hotel (normal opening hours) with bus stop outside for 264 to Bath
(half-hourly services, hourly on Sundays).

This walk is suggested for those who want a gentle stroll or those
with children who will want to stop and play at frequent intervals. The
more energetic can easily follow the canal side tow-path another 4½
miles into Bath. The first part of this second stretch is in the same
delightful wooded valley. The final mile or two is through the outskirts
of Bath, but the canal's descent into Bath by the twelve locks of the
Widcombe flight (now almost restored) affords magnificent views over

the city. The canal joins the river Avon just behind Bath Spa station.

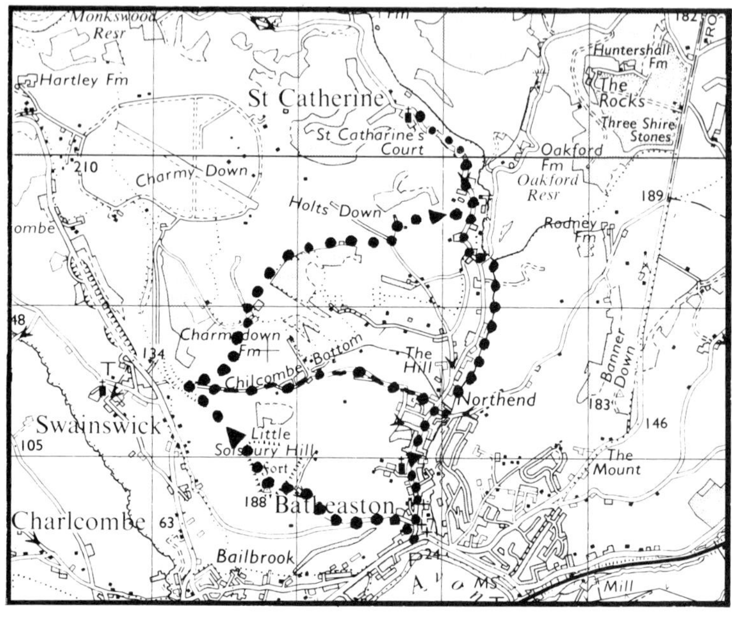

O.S. 172   •—•—• shorter walk

14 LITTLE SOLSBURY HILL AND ST CATHERINE'S VALLEY (7 miles; shorter walk 3½ miles)

Harold Overton

Travel: From Bristol to Bath by Bristol Bus or British Rail; thence by Bristol Buses to Batheaston (numerous services). Motorists: Park just off A4 at Batheaston. (Parking in village proper – uphill – very difficult.)
Refreshments: Mead Tea Gardens, St Catherine's.
[Map: Ordnance Survey 1:50,000 Series, Sheet 172.]

From the main A4 road (G.R. 777675) take the signposted turning for Northend and St Catherine's. Immediately afterwards take the turning on left (marked 'Single track road with passing places'). After half a mile fork right to the gate on to Little Solsbury Hill. The hilltop, now National Trust property, is shown on the map as a 'fort', and is commonly called Solsbury Camp. It is in fact the site of an Iron Age village occupied by the Ancient Britons around 300 to 100 BC. The magnificent views over and around Bath suggest that the inhabitants had plenty of early warning of enemies approaching. On most days, looking to the south, you can see the plume of smoke from the cement factory at Westbury (Wilts.) close by the White Horse, 12 miles away as the crow flies.

On the rounded open hilltop it is not easy to see just where the direct onward path goes. The easiest plan (and a very pleasant one) is to walk up to the National Trust sign and then continue to the left round the edge of the top rampart until you can see not far below a three-armed green public footpath signpost. This is in almost the same line as Charmydown Farm on the opposite hilltop but a little to the left. (You will, in fact, come to that farm later on.) Take the clear path down to the signpost and climb over the stile into the field below. Here the path first veers left, then hugs the right-hand hedge, into a short stretch of green lane, thence over another stile into a field which is subject to ploughing. Skirt along the right-hand hedge and then pass through a wicket-gate to take the clear track down towards two farm sheds.

At this point, you can, if you wish, shorten the walk to about 3½ miles by going through the small gate between the sheds into a green lane and so along the valley (Chilcombe Bottom). You will pass a small reservoir of the Bath City Waterworks, to an asphalt road, eventually

turning right and dropping down to Batheaston. You will have missed
St Catherine's but still have had a pleasant walk.

To continue the main walk, instead of passing between the farm
sheds, go through the gate on the left of the left-hand shed, and straight
up the slope to the gap in the hedge. This is marked by two wooden
posts, which may or may not have a piece of iron railing propped
against them. (In this part of the country contraptions doing duty for
gates or stiles on paths sometimes vary from the casual to the difficult
by way of the eccentric.) Anyway, having passed through the gap, turn
right, take the level path alongside the hedge until you reach a public
footpath signpost in the hedge. Follow its pointer straight up the slope
amongst the bracken (not up the dip full of blackberry bushes a little
further on) to reach a good stile with another signpost. Walk straight up
the field ahead (keeping a little to the left of the line of telephone wires)
up to the right-hand corner and go through the wide gap in the double
hedge. This may sometimes be closed by barbed wire which can be
lifted aside and then replaced. (It's not an intentional obstruction, just
an 'economy model' gate!) Now make towards the top telephone pole
ahead, then veer left to another footpath signpost at the edge of a road,
which you can reach by unhitching one of the posts holding a section
of barbed wire fence; kindly replace, of course. Turn right along the
road to reach Charmydown Farm.

Enter the farmyard, but turn left just before the barn and so into a
field. The path now hugs the right-hand hedge above a wood through
two grass fields, then over another liable to ploughing. Climbing over a
locked gate, continue into the next grassy field, still keeping on the
right-hand edge until you reach a shed for storing hay. Now veer
slightly to the left to a gate in the stone wall at the narrow end of the
field, and so into a lane. Once in the lane, turn right and almost
immediately left over an open triangle of grass towards a house, just
before which there is a grassy track heading straight down the hill.
Carry on down this track; it is a public bridleway, despite all the bits
and pieces of equipment, tools and the like lying around. After a while
the track becomes enclosed by trees and bushes, providing welcome
shade in summer, before reaching the road at St Catherine's. Now look a
little to the right, and across the road you will see a sign for the Mead
Tea Gardens, which may give you an idea.

If desired, you can now walk up the road for half a mile or so to
view St Catharine's Court and the church. (Yes, curiously, the village is
St Catherine with two 'e's, but the Court prefers an 'a' in the middle.)
St Catherine, by the way, is the patron saint of Bath. Her ancient

St Catherine's Church

church, largely rebuilt around 1490, has some interesting stained glass
and a notable monument of 1631 to William Blanchard and his family.
The Court (not open to the public) is an elegant Tudor building once
owned by Sir John Harington, inventor of the water-closet. Unfortunately for Sir John, he once entertained Queen Elizabeth I in his other
house at Kelston and, to defray the expenses of her visit, had to sell St
Catharine's Court to William Blanchard. Note also the attractive
terraced garden and the tithe barn or grange nearby.

To return to Batheaston, walk down the road and turn left, then at
once right on to a footpath. The path crosses a stream by a stone
bridge. At the time of writing, the next stile has collapsed, but a slight
diversion to the left avoids the difficulty. From here on there is a succession of good stiles on the path alongside the stream. On again
reaching a road, turn right, over the stream, and up a slight slope to a
T-junction at Northend, where turn left for the road down into
Batheaston.

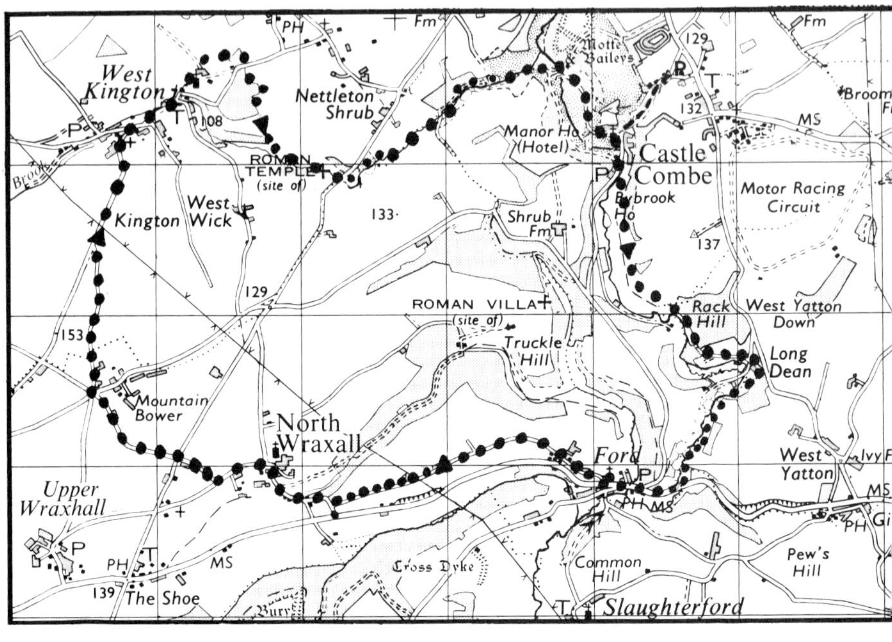

O.S. 173   − − − access route

15 CASTLE COMBE (9 miles)

Kenneth Pinnock

Travel: Bristol Bus No. 335 (not Sundays) from Bristol Bus Station to the North Wraxall turn on the A420. (Note: This is an infrequent service, so check the times carefully before starting). Motorists: Park in lay-bys on A420 near North Wraxall, or use the large free car park on the edge of Castle Combe off B4040 (G.R. 846778), and walk a short distance down into the village to 'break into' the route from there. Refreshments: Pubs in Castle Combe and Ford.
[Map: Ordnance Survey 1:50,000 Series, Sheet 173.]

The lush countryside of West Wiltshire adjoining the new county of Avon offers some very attractive and easy walking through almost unspoilt villages linked by ancient paths. This is such a walk; we visit five pretty villages, including Castle Combe, which is featured on innumerable calendars and was once voted 'England's prettiest village'. Although not everyone would agree with this distinction, it is a 'must' for anyone visiting this part of the county for the first time. Castle Combe achieved additional fame in 1966 when it was used as the location for the filming of part of 'The Story of Dr Doolittle'.

From the bus-stop turn left off the A420 into North Wraxall, noting the tiny schoolroom on your right just inside the village. Bear left and soon afterwards ignore the right turn just past the church. Continue westwards for about a quarter of a mile and then turn right to the cross-roads at G.R. 811751. The crossing road is the old Roman Fosse Way, which we shall rejoin later. Continue straight over the cross-roads to a junction of 5 roads and a stony track. Follow the latter past some houses, after which it becomes an attractive green lane, meeting a minor road at G.R. 806765. Turn right here along the road towards West Kington (note the unusual 'Sheep and Lamb' weather-vane on the barn at the fine old farm on the outskirts of the village). Follow the Castle Combe/Nettleton/Burton road down into the village and there cross the stream. Climb the steep little lane to the left of the old post office, to enter a field at the top, with the church to the right. Now make for a stile in the hedge by an electricity pole just past the farm (G.R. 813777), and cut across the field, bearing slightly right to make for a hand-gate at the tip of the wood on the far side at G.R. 816778, thence along the edge of this wood to join the road via a second, similar gate at G.R. 816777. (Alternatively, follow the short cart track left of the farmyard to the service road, which you can follow to the road through a gate near a cottage, before turning left to arrive at G.R. 816777.) Pass through the opposite hand-gate, and follow the irregular edge of woodland along a clear path which is not shown on the map. Down in the corner at the end of this field, ignore the right-hand field gate, but go through the facing hand-gate at G.R. 817773. Follow the right edge of the next field for about 25 yards to follow a slightly descending grassy path to a hidden facing wicket gate among the trees, and so down along a rutted track into a lovely valley at G.R. 818771.

Turn left along this valley, following the clear stream, which we shall encounter through the remainder of this walk. As you near the road and bridge, note the site of a Roman temple, marked by a wooden stake. This was the scene of extensive digging some years ago, and several 'finds' are now in Bristol Museum. The road through the gate is the old Fosse Way again, which you will remember you crossed earlier. Follow it for about 70 yards to leave it through a wooden hand-gate on the right, and so along the gradually descending path to follow the

Castle Combe

stream along to the picturesque Nettleton Ford (G.R. 830774). Do not cross the ancient clapper bridge, but continue with the stream on your right to Nettleton Hill. Enter Castle Combe Park through a hand-gate on the right and follow the waymarked footpath, curving soon to a large stone bridge, obviously built for wheeled traffic. Still keeping to the waymarked path, follow alongside a wire fence to the right and, later, a wall, to a stile leading on to a tiny lane into Castle Combe. (If you parked your car in the car park at G.R. 846778 previously mentioned, you will have walked the short distance down into the village to pick up the route from here.) Continue down the street and over the bridge, then cross the second of two more bridges over the stream and turn immediately right through a gate. Carry on to the stile ahead, thence on a waymarked path on the left of a hedge, gradually rising up the side of the valley. Later, this path runs along the steep hillside, from which the stream below can not only be seen, but heard! Continue straight on, soon descending along a cart track to Long Dean, with its attractively restored cottages. Turn right at the crossing, then cross a stone stile on the left on the near side of the bridge. Follow the stream, which is the same one you have followed for the last few miles. Very soon the path crosses and recrosses it, and continues clearly along to join the main Chippenham-Bristol road. Turn right along this road for a quarter of a mile to Ford, where there is a bus-stop opposite the church. Otherwise, complete the circle by turning right along the lane just past the church, marked 'The Malt House', to reach the starting point of the walk in 1¼ miles.

Teal Fm
Avon
Grove Fm
Manor Fm
Thornhill Fm
Hare Street Fm
Weir
MS
Langley Ho
LANGLEY BURRELL
WITHOUT
Kellaways
East Tytherton
Barrow Fm
Langley Burrell
P
Peckingell
Gaston's Fm
Catbrook
P
Bremhill Grove
Pew Hill
Manor Fm
West Tytherton
Bremhill Wick
Rawlings Fm
Stokes Fm
Monument
Coll
New Leaze Fm
Scott's Mill Fm
Inscribed Stone
Wick Hill
Monkton Ho
Harden's Fm
Cse of old rly
Bencroft Hill
Nature Trail
Bremh
Host
Stanley
Dumb Post (PH)
Hither Fm
Haze
Sewage Wks
Cemy
Jay's Fm
Pound Fm
Mill
Stanley Abbey Fm
Ratf
P E W S H A M
Abbey (site of)
Forest Fm
Forest Gate Fm
Close Wood
Studley
MS
Middle Lodge Fm
MS
Derry
PH
T PH
Great Lodge Fm
Woods
Rumsey Ho
Lower Lodge Fm
Cocklemore Brook
Pewsham Ho
Derry Hill
Bassett's Moor
Inn
Golden Gates
Queenwood
The Osprey
Horse Copse
Pigsty Copse
River Marden

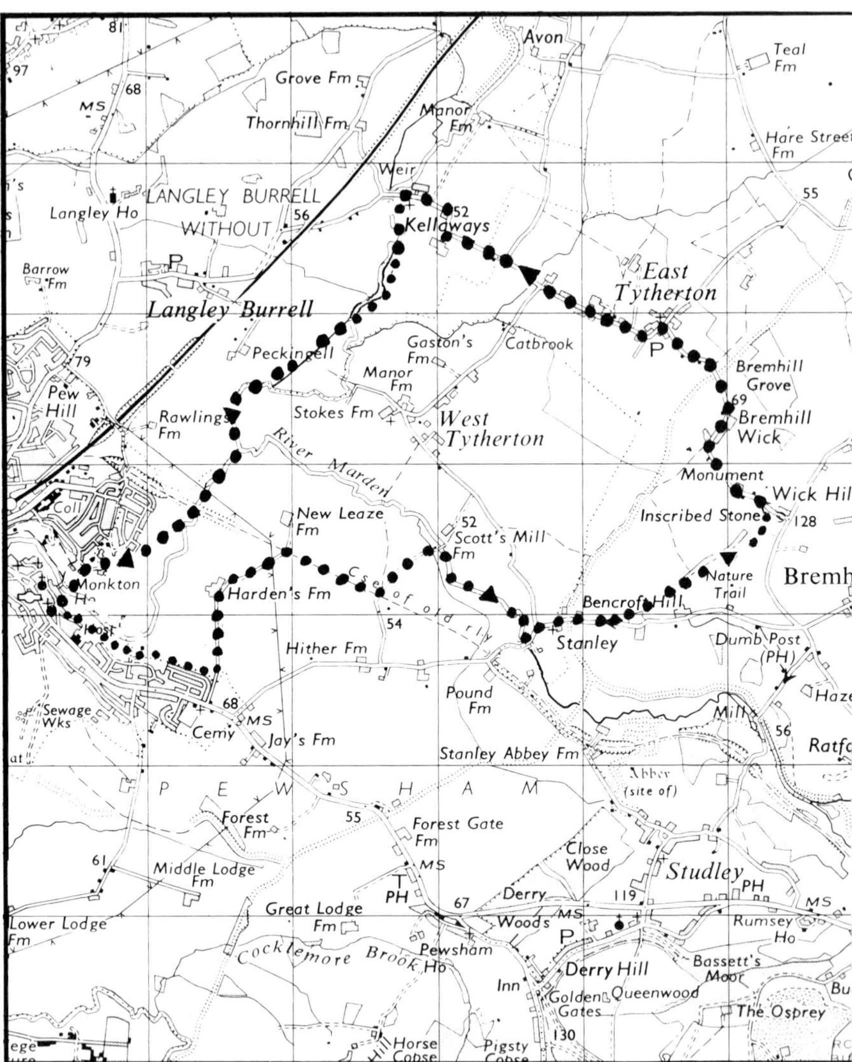

O.S. 173

16 MAUD HEATH'S CAUSEWAY FROM CHIPPENHAM
(9 miles)

Kenneth Pinnock

Travel: From Bristol and Bath, British Rail to Chippenham, or Bristol Bus No. 335 (weekdays only) and 231 from Bristol and Nos. 232 (infrequent) and 465 (weekdays only) from Bath. Motorists: Plentiful car parking in the town.
Refreshments: No facilities en route, so packed food is advisable. Ample facilities in Chippenham.
[Map: Ordnance Survey 1:50,000 Series, Sheet 173.]

Maud Heath was a market-woman who lived in Langley Burrell village, near Chippenham, in the fifteenth century. Tradition says that she found the roads of that time impassable for most of the year, and so to improve the one between Wick Hill and Chippenham Clift, she left her life savings in perpetuity at £8 per annum, which must have been a huge sum then. This ramble gives us the opportunity to see some of the original Causeway, as well as to obtain some wide views from Wick Hill over the North Wiltshire countryside.

Start from the War Memorial in the town centre, and go along the A4 in the direction of Calne for a short distance before turning left along Ladd's Lane, which is the one just past the Causeway Methodist Church. Turn first right (The Butts), then left along Baydon Lane, soon leaving the surfaced path after some wooden railings to follow a path across the meadow straight ahead to the Sea Cadets' huts at G.R. 929727. The Wiltshire Avon runs on your left. Climb the bank ahead and continue in roughly the same direction around the edge of a large pasture field at the rear of modern houses, to join a crossing farm road at the end. Follow this left straight past Harden's Farm as far as a disused railway track (the old Chippenham/Calne branch line), which you now follow right for about half a mile, to a transverse metal gate at G.R. 946731. Here enter the field on the left and follow a rutted cart track through the fields towards Scott's Mill Farm. After climbing an iron gate, bear right in front of the ruined creeper-covered mill, to follow an obvious path alongside the River Marden (which is a tributary of the Wiltshire Avon) and so ahead to join the road to the river bridge (G.R. 956727). Here turn left, and soon fork right along the Bremhill road. Note the white-painted railings outside Stanley Bridge Farm, almost half-way up the hill. This is where the old Wilts. and Berks. Canal used to pass under the road. It is difficult to realise now that this canal was in use as recently as just over sixty years ago. Continue up to the top of the hill, there to join a path through a metal gate set at an angle in the hedge on the left at G.R. 964729. Now, keeping the fence and, soon, some woodland on your left, continue straight through the fields to the road at the top of Wick Hill. Notice the inscribed stone just here, marking one end of Maud Heath's Causeway. The impressive monument across the field on the opposite side of the road is topped by her statue, and was erected in 1838. A path leads across to it. This is an ideal spot for a picnic if the weather and visibility are suitable, as the views from this vantage point of about 125 metres (410 ft.) are superb.

Return to the road, and go downhill, to reach the pretty little village of East Tytherton. Continue through by turning left and then right, and

Maud Heath's Causeway

follow the quiet country road beyond for about 1¼ miles, past the tiny church at Kellaways. Soon after this you come upon the raised part of the original Causeway alongside the road. You can walk along the top of it above the 46 arches. The quaint sundial, dated 1698, on the other side of the road near the river bridge, tells the story of Maud Heath's bequest.

Descend steps on the left to the bank of the Avon, and follow the path which at first runs along it. At the end of the first field it leaves the bank to continue from the gate in the left corner (G.R. 947754), then along the left hedge in the next field to another gate in the far left corner at G.R. 946752, where it rejoins the river. Now follow the right edge of the third field with the river, to cross it via the concrete bridge at G.R. 944749. From near the wartime pillbox there is a straight drain, cutting across the large river bend, which it meets again at G.R. 939745. Follow this drain on its left side (not the other side as on the map), to a crossing track on the other side of a facing field gate at the end of the field (G.R. 941747). Now you can easily change over to the other side of the drain and continue in the same direction to its junction with the river.

The footpath shown on the map from this point and running south of Rawlings Farm to the outskirts of Chippenham is not easy to find. An easier route is to divert slightly right to the facing field gate, and cross the short field to a half-hidden low stile in the bushes on the far side. Now follow the winding path to the left through the scrub, soon to arrive at a wooden stile right at the water's edge. Continue along the clear path along the river bank, straight to the old railway bridge support at G.R. 933737, and so to the edge of a new housing estate. Rejoin the river bank, and follow the path to an iron gate to the left corner of the facing hedge, where you enter Monkton Park. Cut diagonally right to a stile in the far corner of the crossing fence, then follow the edge of a small golf course to the bridge over the river at G.R. 924732. You can now get back to your starting point via the back streets of Chippenham.

The spired Church of St Andrew nearby is large, beautiful and well worth a visit if time permits. Of special interest are the Prynne monument and the superb rood screen erected in 1921 to commemorate the 129 men of the district who gave their lives in the 1914-18 War. This merits very close study. There is also some very lovely stained glass.

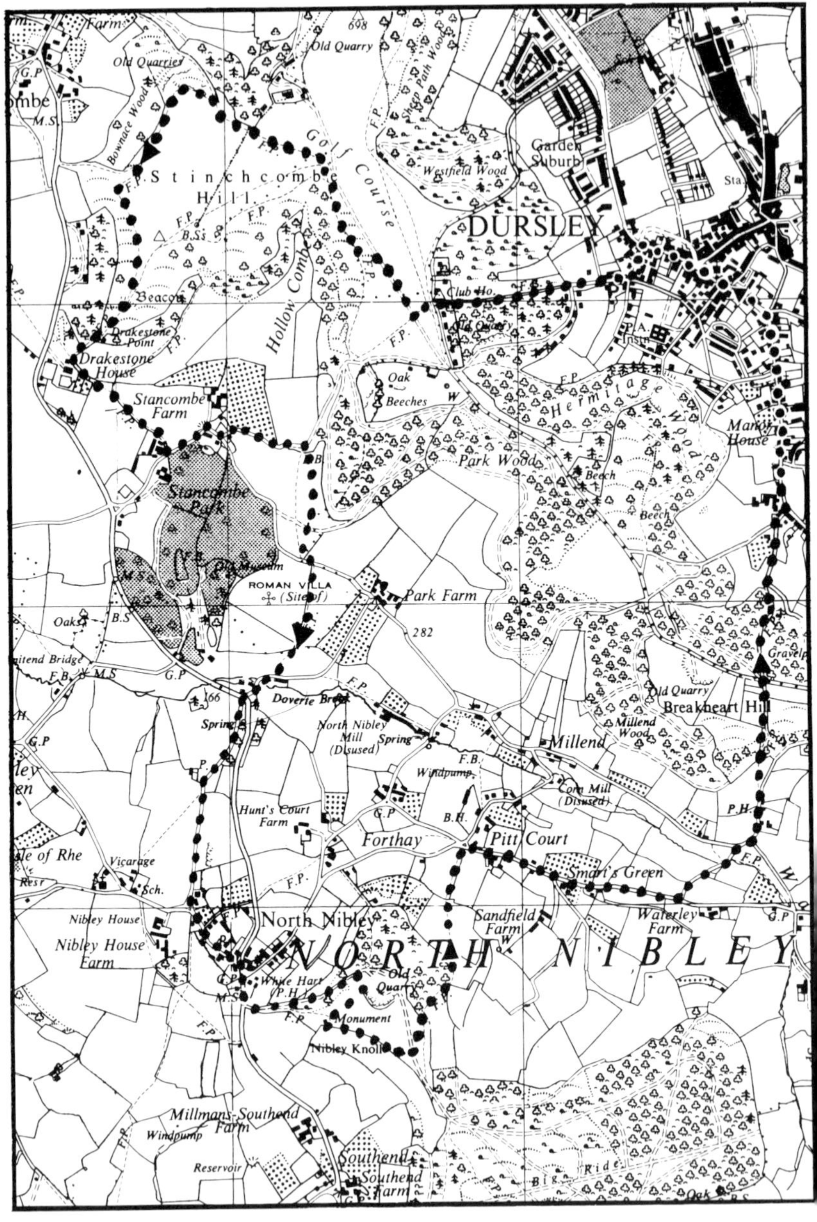

O.S. Sheet ST 79

17 DURSLEY, STINCHCOMBE HILL AND THE TYNDALE MONUMENT (7¼ miles)

Tony Drake

Travel: Bristol Bus No. 525/6 from Bristol or Gloucester to Dursley. May Lane. Motorists: Car park in Hill Road, Dursley.
Refreshments: Various pubs in Dursley; Black Horse at North Nibley; New Inn, near Breakheart Hill.
[Map: Ordnance Survey 1:50,000 Series, Sheet 162, or 1:25,000 Series, Sheet ST 79 (latter is much to be preferred).]

This walk takes you over a particularly scenic segment of the beautiful southern Cotswolds. The first 4 miles follow parts of the route of the Cotswold Way, the long-distance path from Chipping Campden to Bath (the major responsibility for which rests with the Gloucestershire County Council), and these are generally well signed and waymarked. The Way's particular waymark is a small white circular spot on signposts etc., but you will also encounter squat, coloured directional arrows — yellow for footpath and blue for bridleway — as recommended by the Countryside Commission for use on rights of way in England and Wales generally. This is a hilly walk, so come well shod and take your time over it. In fact people who are elderly or not very fit would be advised not to attempt this quite strenuous expedition.

Alight from the bus at Dursley bus station, May Lane, turn right into Hill Road and go steeply uphill for about 200 yards. (If coming by car the Hill Road car park could hardly be more convenient. There are toilets there too.) When the road turns sharply left continue ahead on to a signposted track into the woods (G.R. 753981), being very careful to fork *left* on the ascending path just beyond the signpost. Climb steadily up through the beechwoods to emerge on to a golf course. Bear slightly left across the grass to a waymarked post and then right on to the tarmac road which cuts across the course. Near the parking area half-way along, look to your left for a distant view of your objective, the Tyndale Monument.

As the road veers away in the right, fork left on to a clear track (marked by a blue arrow) and then, as this track begins to descend, fork left on to a footpath (yellow arrow). Note the old mounting stone for horse-riders at this point. The path now begins to turn gently leftwards round the edge of Stinchcombe Hill and the golf course to bring

you to a delightful little stone shelter with seats. From here there are
marvellous views over the Vale of Severn, with the great wide river
stretching across it. Ancient Berkeley Castle lies right ahead whilst to
your left in the distance is the new Severn Bridge. The path continues
to the south-western corner of the Hill at Drakestone Point with another
view of the Monument. Having now left the Cotswold Way descend the
steep 'nose' of the hill. Do not, however, follow the obvious way down,
which is uncomfortably steep, but traverse left, to enter the wood
below at a gap some 30 yards to the left of the obvious way down the
'nose'. The path leads down through the wood to a stile, with Drakestone House beyond. Turn left over the stile along an enclosed path.
Cross another stile and continue south-eastwards on a field-path with a
fence on your right, eventually coming out on to a minor road by a
farm via a stone 'squeeze' stile beside the gate.

Turn left along the road, and as it bends right, with another farm on
your left, look for a track going off left. Turn down here, with a house
on your right, and ascend gently, with trees on either side. After
about 350 yards you will rejoin the Cotswold Way at some steps
leading down the sides of the deep gulley alongside a large gas main on
the right of the track. Negotiate these steps and enter the adjoining
field over a stile. Keeping roughly parallel with the woods on your left
go across this field to a stile in the fence on your right, climb over this
and bear left to climb another stile in the hedge. Turn left here into a
narrow road and shortly afterwards take a signposted path off it to the
right, over a stile. This path runs alongside a hedge, goes over 3 more
stiles and finally descends to another minor road. Turn right here
through a little hamlet built around the Doverie Brook and cross over
the B4060 road into a good, clear hedge-lined track (Lowerhouse Lane)
which takes you straight into the village of North Nibley near the
church.

The Tyndale Monument stands high above the village just to the
south-east and is approached up a steep track leading off the B4060
(where there is a sign and a board with instructions about gaining entry
to the Monument). The track, which in wet weather gets muddy and
slippery, lies in a rather impressive, if gloomy, steep-sided, tree-lined
combe. Near the top it is necessary to deviate from the official right of
way and to follow the sign directing you sharp right. You eventually
emerge into the open, puffing and blowing, via a stile, with the Monument straight ahead looking very impressive. You will probably think
the effort well worth while when you see the view. The great stone
tower, built in 1866, commemorates William Tyndale, the great re-

Tyndale Monument

ligious reformer and translator of the Bible, who is believed to have
been born in North Nibley. He was put to death for his activities in
1536.

With the Monument behind you walk along the edge of the escarpment, with a fence on your right, for about 250 yards and then, parting
company with the Cotswold Way, swing leftwards across the field and
descend towards a little clump of silver birches standing in front of the
woods which line the eastern edge of the field. Go straight into the
woods by a gate and follow a clear path downhill, crossing a forest
road, to a field gate. Bear left through here into the field with the
woods on your left and a fine view on your right. Pass through the next
gate and descend across the next field, at the bottom of which go
through a gate into a wide track. At the end of this go out through
another gate and turn right into a minor road. Continue along the road,
past Pitt Court, and in about half a mile fork left down a very narrow
road to reach the isolated but charmingly situated New Inn, with
panoramic views from its garden. Leave the lane and climb the bank
opposite the inn to follow a path running parallel with the lane at first
and then climbing steeply across the corner of a field and into a wood
via a stile.

You are now well and truly on your way up Breakheart Hill, but do not despair! It is all downhill once you get to the top, from which there is quite a good view. On emerging from the wood follow the straight wide gravel track ahead. Cross straight over a minor road on to a pleasant path descending through trees which brings you out to the southern outskirts of Dursley. Follow the road into Dursley and enjoy your walk through this picturesque old town back to your starting point.

123
Howley
MS
Brackenbury Ditches
Fort
Bournstream
NT
195
Wimley Hill
Tyley Bottom
Coombe Hill
Coombe
Cannon's Court Fm
Strip Lynchets
Wotton Hill
Strip Lynchets
Holywell
Bradley
Burrough Hill Fm
Merlin Haven
Warren Ho
Newark Park
Long Barrow
Bushford Br
MS
37
Wotton-under-Edge
72
Cemy
Tor Hill
Yew
Sch
Hawpark Fm
Little Tor Hill
Wortley Hill
Ozle
Textile Mill
Leys Fm
Grange Fm
Kingswood
P.
T
Wortley
56
Cemy
Nind Fm
54
Park Fm
Alderley
Alderley Wood
Upper Barns Fm
Alderley
Winner Hill
od
64
Highwood Fm
Newmills

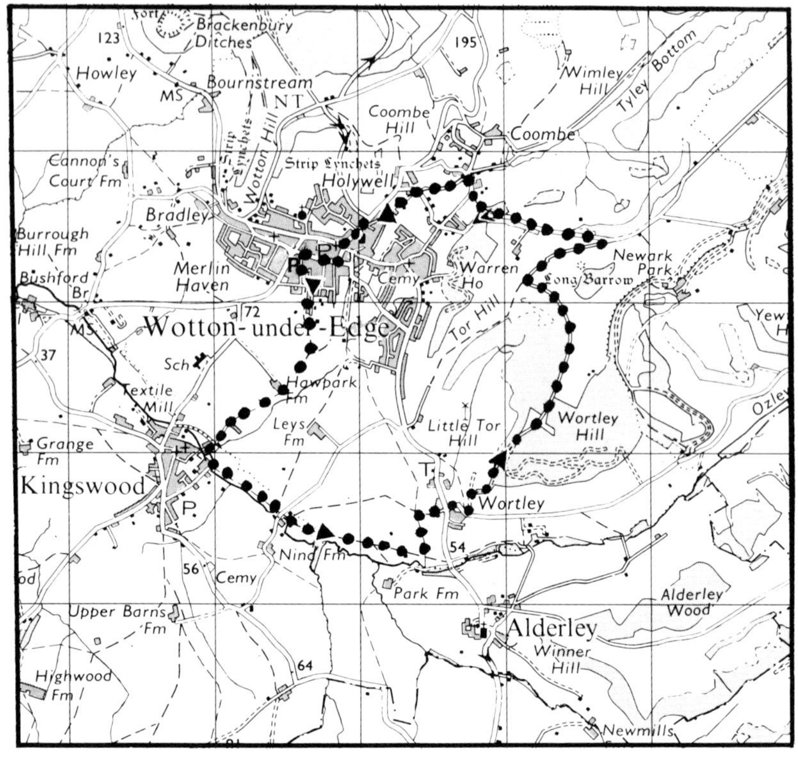

O.S. 162

18 WOTTON-UNDER-EDGE, KINGSWOOD AND BLACKQUARRIES HILL (6 miles)

Cyril Trenfield

*Travel: From Bristol or Gloucester by Bristol Bus No. 526 to
Wotton-under-Edge. From Bristol or Stroud by Bristol Bus No. 400.
Motorists: Car park in Market Street, Wotton-under-Edge.
Refreshments: Available in Wotton-under-Edge and Kingswood.
[Map: Ordnance Survey 1:50,000 Series, Sheet 162.]*

This circular walk is based on the fascinating old town of Wotton-under-Edge in the southernmost range of the Cotswolds. Once a busy centre of cloth-weaving this former market town is well worth looking round, if you have time, either before or after the walk. The Parish Church of St Mary's, started early in the fourteenth century, is spaciously imposing, with a lofty impressive tower. The organ comes from St Martin-in-the-Fields, London, and was originally given to that church by George I. The town's Grammar School was founded in 1382, and one of its pupils was Edward Jenner, the discoverer of vaccination. Another notable former resident of the town was Isaac Pitman, the shorthand pioneer.

From the bus-stop (G.R. 758934) walk downhill towards the war memorial (on an island in the middle of the road) and turn right up Church Street, noting the quaint old almshouses (1634) on the left-hand side. At the end turn right into Long Street, the main street with its many shops. Just before the overhanging Queen Victoria Jubilee clock turn left along Market Street and at the end veer diagonally left across the open space, once the site of the market and now a car park, to a pedestrian access in the corner with two concrete posts. Turn left briefly into narrow Symn Lane and then right along a clear footpath signposted 'Public Footpath — Kingswood'.

Now keep to the left field boundary, passing a children's recreational area, and at the end of some buildings on the left cross a narrow stile and head for another stile at the bottom corner of the next field. Cross this and continue alongside a hedge on the left to cross yet another stile, adjacent to Hawpark Farm, on the right. After crossing two further fields you come to a stony lane leading up to a row of houses. Continue in the same direction past the house frontages and along the access road that leads up to a footbridge over a tributary of the Little

Avon River.

Over the bridge you meet up with a metalled path. The route now turns left along this, but before you follow it I suggest you make a short detour by forking right instead into Kingswood. This former weaving village contains interesting relics of its industrial past, e.g. old mills and housing in a variety of styles for the mill workers. A Cistercian Abbey was established here in 1139, but regrettably the only remaining evidence you can see today is the fifteenth-century gateway. The village church dates from 1723.

Retrace your steps to the path junction near the bridge and take the metalled path referred to above, passing an old mill, now a printing works, and cross an access road to enter via a wicket gate another metalled path alongside the river bank (to the right). This eventually becomes a meadow-path and crosses a narrow metalled lane. Now look for the signpost 'Footpath: Wortley' and, crossing one stile and another soon after, traverse a field which has been split into paddocks via two yellow iron gates. On meeting the river bank do not proceed further to the field extremity but turn to the left hedge to cross a stile, soon followed by another stile between an oak tree and an ash tree.

The route now lies left of the overhead electricity line, through a gap in the hedge towards a makeshift wooden stile. The field ahead is normally cropped with root vegetables, so the best way to discern the path across it is to proceed to the second pole and then veer slightly right to reach an iron gate at the field corner.

Instead of crossing the meadow beyond with its fine oak tree, turn left inside it alongside the wire fence and go through a wooden field gate into the next field, and cross it by setting a direction slightly left of the distant round-shaped hill. This should lead you to a rather inconspicuous stile in the hedge. Do not cross this stile but turn right, with the hedge to your left, to make your exit through a white gate, past a house in local stone and along its drive into a road. This is Wortley.

Cross the road and walk up the opposite lane between some houses for approximately 100 yards. After rounding a double bend fork left via a field gate on to a track signposted 'Footpath — Blackquarries Hill'. From this track you will get fine views of Alderley village and the southern Cotswold escarpment. Note from the signpost that you are now on a section of the Cotswold Way (see Walk No. 17).

After 50 yards turn right through a waymarked field gate, to join a clear path that becomes a track as it wends its way up between steep banks and forestry plantation to the top of Blackquarries Hill. The track continues along the ridge and eventually joins the road for

Wotton-under-Edge. The extensive views you can enjoy from this
section of the route include the Tyndale Monument, the Vale of
Severn and the Forest of Dean.

Turn left down the road, taking special care to note the Warren
Farm access road on your left. Still keeping to the descending road, at
the *sixth* telegraph pole from the Warren Farm road veer right from the
road, as it steeply descends round a left bend, and go along a sort of
drainage channel at the clearing. This quickly becomes an obvious
footpath down the steep hillside between high trees and overgrown
hedges and meets up with a small metalled road. Turn right here down a
larger road a few yards ahead, to the bottom of the hill. This is Coombe.

At the stream turn left along the obvious path that keeps close to its
bank, cross a small road, with the Parish Church of Wotton-under-Edge
now in sight, and eventually come into Valley Road and join up with
the main road. Here turn left past the church and so on to the town
centre and the buses by way of the War Memorial.

Wortley

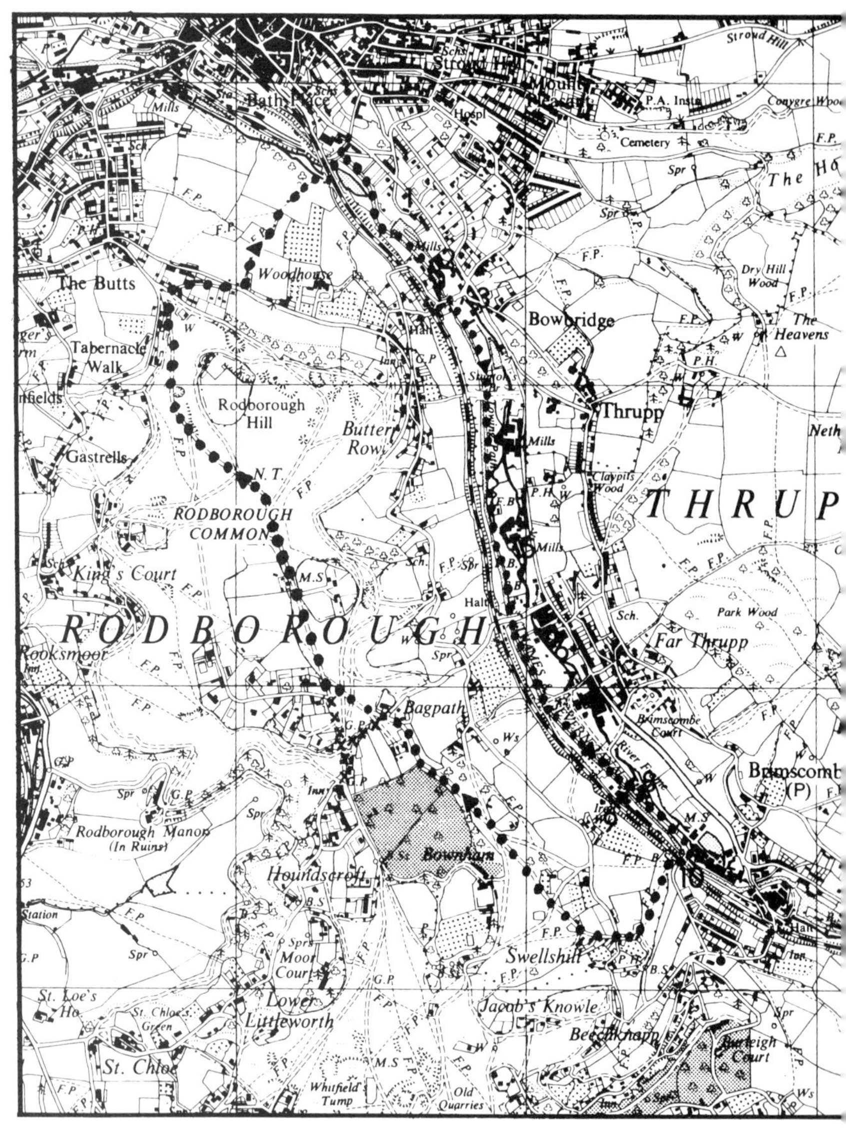

O.S. Sheet SO 80 ✗✗✗✗ diversion

19 RODBOROUGH COMMON AND THE GOLDEN VALLEY (4 miles)

Tony Jones

Travel: From Bristol to Stroud by British Rail or Bristol Bus Nos. 400 and 830. From Gloucester to Stroud by British Rail, or Bristol Bus Nos. 556 and 558. From Cheltenham to Stroud by British Rail, or Bristol Bus Nos. 563 and 564. Motorists: Large car park off London Road, Stroud, quarter of a mile south-east of railway station (G.R. 853049), or use the various car parks on Rodborough Common (being careful not to park more than 15 yards from the road). Refreshments: Ample facilities in Stroud, also Bear Inn, near Rodborough Common.
[Map: Ordnance Survey 1:50,000 Series, Sheet 162 or 1:25,000 Series Sheet SO 80 (preferable).]

This circular walk takes you through two distinct landscapes, the Golden Valley with the Thames-Severn Canal and the Rodborough Common area of the Cotswold Hills. Whilst described from a starting point on the outskirts of Stroud, the route offers a choice of access points — from the many bus stops along the valley floor, or from the car parks in the area of Rodborough Common.

From the centre of Stroud follow the A419 Cirencester road (London Road) south-eastwards for about half a mile, with the railway line on your right. Soon after passing the large car park you will come to a bus and coach depot, also on your right, and at the end of this turn right down a tarmacadam track. You will shortly come to the start of the route, an old iron bridge over what remains of the Thames-Severn Canal (G.R. 853047).

Stand on this bridge and take the opportunity of savouring the atmosphere of industrial dereliction which it affords. What a change from the scene existing in the eighteen-hundreds when the canal provided the main means of transport for the area! Water has governed man's use of this valley from the earliest times; springs dictated the sites of earliest settlements whilst fords influenced the routes of tracks and roads. The river provided power for the original mills, mainly for corn grinding and cloth manufacture, and the water itself had qualities making it particularly suitable for fulling — the felting of the cloth. Most of the original mills have long since disappeared, but their sites have had a continuous industrial use, many today forming small industrial estates with a wide diversity of industry. The encircled numbers on the map identify the sites of mills, both past and present, and these sites are described at the corresponding numbers in the text.

Retrace your steps off the bridge, turn right and descend to the towpath. Between this point and Bowbridge it is possible to deviate from the path and see the once important weirs and millponds, now quiet backwaters, and the haunt of all kinds of wild life. Certain stretches of the canal are in fact now recognised as valuable nature conservation areas. A word of warning is, however, necessary. Although the canal is no longer in use some sections still contain deep water, so take care!

Arundell Mill (1) in the mid-eighteenth century was important for wool and its dyeing, yet one hundred years later was manufacturing artificial manure! Nearby, the Eagle Spinning Mills (2) produced woollen products and, further from the canal, the Newcombe or Sands Mill was noted for leather and later, wool. In the seventeenth century the Bowbridge Mills and dye houses (3) formed a corn and wool complex, and an upholstery works was also noted on the site.

Beyond Bowbridge you will notice evidence of reclamation work being carried out by the active canal preservation society. A mammoth task comfronts them.

Stanton Bridge is a suitable point at which to pause and appreciate the importance of the valley to man as a communications route — canal, railway and road. The busy A419 only just above the valley floor illustrates the importance and shortage of flat land. This is just one of many steep-sided valleys in the area, important for through traffic and yet having their own network of tracks linking their once flourishing cottage industries. Even today many of the new factories are small concerns with work forces below fifty.

Beyond the bridge is the site of Stafford Mills (4), the first mills in Gloucestershire to have power looms. The site of Griffins Mill (5) has seen many changes, from grain and wool in the sixteenth century to timber, and, during this century, aircraft manufacture! This area with its lattice-work iron footbridge illustrates the diversity of crafts that have been carried out — not only textiles, but the actual machinery for the mills, and even lawn-mowers have been important products.

Pass the next bridge to the sites of two famous mills — Ham Mills (7) noted for carpets and wool products and still manufacturing textiles, and the Phoenix Ironworks. Further canal restoration work will be seen here, and one wonders what effect this will have as one comes to a relatively modern factory built virtually over the course of the canal.

Numbers (8) and (9) are the sites of the Gough and Hope Mills complex and the Canal Ironworks, the former having a varied history of fulling, grain, silk and engineering dating back to the mid-sixteenth century.

Leave the canal at the next bridge, passing the site of Brimscombe Mills (10), another mill complex of the same period. These mills were important in the wool trade for over four hundred years. After crossing the canal bridge pass under the railway bridge and through a hunting-gate on the right. Climb steadily up the tarmacadam footpath, passing a cottage before going through another hunting-gate. Continue on between stone-built cottages, over the cross tracks and continue climbing until the cottage 'Glenview' is reached. Immediately beyond this cottage a grassy bank affords an excellent resting place with superb views over the Golden Valley to Thrupp, Brimscombe and Chalford.

Rested, continue the gradual climb round to the right, the track eventually leading to open common land. Civilisation appears ahead in the form of a petrol sign! Depending on the time of day and one's creature needs a short deviation to the Bear Inn is recommended. Extensive views of Woodchester and the Nailsworth Valley can be seen from the adjacent National Trust land.

Turning one's back on the Bear pass the garage and continue along the road side — or over the Common until the tower of Rodborough Fort comes into sight. If necessary, carefully cross the road at the sharp right-hand bend. (The 'private track — no access' notice refers to cars.) Follow the track round to the right, eventually arriving at Rodborough Fort, a famous landmark and viewpoint but of little historical significance. It was built as an eighteenth-century house and its grounds are now a Caravan Club site.

With the fort on your right make your way down the grassy slopes, cross the road and descend Dark Lane, a steep tarmacadam lane between stone walls. On reaching a T-junction turn right for about 12 yards before going left through a spring gate and descending through a pasture field. Keeping the hedge on your right continue losing height, go through a gap in the hedge, then over a stile and go ever downward until a good track is reached. Follow this to the right still descending.

During this descent you are afforded glimpses of history through the somewhat haphazard development that has ebbed and flowed according to the prosperity of the mills. Much of the new residential development is high on the valley side, whilst the older dwellings are mixed with the industrial sites along the valley floor.

On reaching a wire fence continue to the right along the track. Soon

Rodborough Fort

you will hear the sound of running water — the River Frome — which is crossed by a footbridge. Overhead looms the viaduct carrying the Gloucester-Swindon Railway, the final nail in the coffin of the canal as a commercial enterprise. Follow the path under the viaduct and so come back to the canal bridge and your starting point.

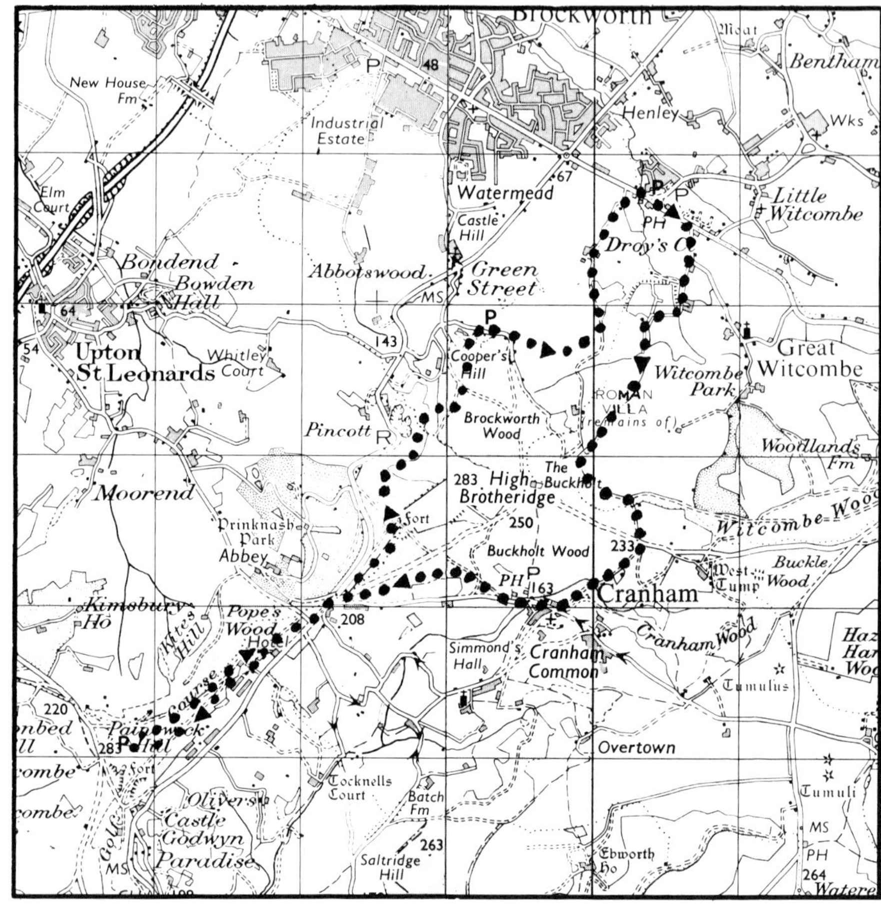

O.S. 162 and 163

20 CRANHAM AND THE HILL ABOVE PARADISE
(9 miles; shorter walk 5 miles)

Fred Whitwood

Travel: British Rail to Gloucester; thence Bristol Bus Nos. 554 and 555 to Witcombe, Twelve Bells Inn. From Cheltenham/Stroud use Bristol Bus No. 564 to Brockworth, Cross Hands Inn; then short walk along A417 to Twelve Bells Inn. (Note: on Sundays no service on 555 whilst 554 runs more frequently then to Cross Hands Inn than to Twelve Bells.) Motorists: Park at Twelve Bells (with landlord's permission) or at the foot of Cooper's Hill or approaches to Painswick Hill.
Refreshments: Twelve Bells Inn, Witcombe; Black Horse Inn, Cranham; Adam and Eve Inn, Paradise.
[Map: Ordnance Survey 1:50,000 Series, Sheets 162 and 163.]

A Roman villa, woodland glades and a superb viewpoint are all to be found on this fine, hilly Cotswold walk. If you prefer a shortened version you can omit the last 4 miles by catching a bus.

From the Twelve Bells (G.R. 904157) take the (Roman) road for Great and Little Witcombe and turn first right off this towards Great Witcombe; and then after about 300 yards right again down a lane between cottages. This becomes a private farm access road and bridleway and bears right, with reservoirs for Gloucester on either side; a noted haunt for waterfowl of all kinds. (Please go quietly along here to avoid disturbing the wild life.) Beyond this peaceful scene a fine arc of fields and rising woods tempts you forward and upward.

Bear left round the perimeter of the southern reservoir to a gate at the end of the access road and continue along the bridleway proper. In wet weather you will doubtless encounter mud, glorious mud, along this short stretch, but before you berate the author for his choice of route think of the reputed beneficial qualities of this inconvenient substance! Continue along this track via a gate and along the left edge of a field, avoiding the lure of an opening off to the left. Near the far end of the field, ignoring two gates close together, go through another one just ahead into the next field and follow the clear grass track across it uphill. Up on your right is the fenced site of the Witcombe Roman villa, with restoration work in progress (at the time of writing). The original stone for this building is believed to have been brought from Italy.

Witcombe Roman villa

Go through the gate at the highest and furthest point in the field, ignoring previous exits, and follow the track up into the woods with tall beeches rising like slender columns and supporting the lofty fan-vaulting of their branches. Bear round to the left above the spring at the head of the stream which helps feed the reservoirs and after about 250 yards fork right on to a path which leads up and out on to a minor road. Turn left along this for about 100 yards and then take the wide track off to the right to a clearing in the wood from which paths fan out in all directions. Take the main, hard-surfaced path leading down towards a house and bear to the right of its grounds as you descend through the woods to a small glade at the bottom of the valley with a stream hurrying along — an attractive spot indeed.

Cross the stream by a footbridge, and the path soon comes to a minor road. Turn right into it and so enter Cranham village. The Black Horse Inn is a few steps along to the left. Continue along the road through the village and at the crest of the hill bear right to rejoin the woodland paths, keeping parallel with and close to the road. Skirt a field between the edge of the wood and the road and then veer left-wards to rejoin the road. Soon afterwards another minor road comes in on your right and shortly after that you come to the Prinknash Corner junction with the A46. (Here you can catch a 564 bus to Stroud, Brockworth or Cheltenham if you do not wish to walk any further.)

Turn left briefly along the A46 and then right on to the Upton St Leonards road, but only a few steps along this turn left on to the path for Painswick Beacon. Take the right-hand fork at the start for a slightly more adventurous way up. The path eventually follows round the right-hand edge of a golf course to reach the summit (283 metres; 928 ft.) with its excellent views towards the Severn, the Forest of Dean, May Hill, the distant Welsh Hills, the Malverns, Bredon Hill and, nearer at hand, Gloucester and Robinswood Hill, whilst behind and below you on the A46 just to the south is the area known as Paradise, traditionally so called by Charles I during the Civil War. It is still a delightful little place today, with its Adam and Eve Inn. (If you prefer you can now make your way down to it quite easily and catch a 564 bus there.)

You now return across the golf course to Prinknash Corner using the wider alternative path. Incidentally, between the Beacon and Cooper's Hill you are on another section of the Cotswold Way (see Walk 17). As you reach the A46 you may catch a glimpse of Prinknash Abbey far below (and of course you will have a further opportunity to catch a bus).

Turn right briefly on to the Cranham road and then look for a narrow concealed path on the left, which should be signposted 'Cooper's Hill', and which soon opens out with a wall on your left. Cross through a ruined gap in the wall and after a short distance follow the path bearing left and descending close to the main road and an entrance to the Abbey. There is a choice of route here. Take the easier path by keeping left at each fork to reach a clearing in the wood, and cross the remains of another wall. Continue through the woods towards Cooper's Hill by a path well marked by arrows. At a break in the woods the path passes between two fields. Re-enter the woods and so climb up to the summit with its maypole and steep slope for the ancient Whitsuntide Cheese Rolling ceremony, with cottages far below looking like small models.

Now descend the hill, taking the easier paths to the left of the Cheese Rolling slope, to the car park. Turn right along the road past the 'Footpath to Brockworth' sign (an alternative way to the Cross Hands Inn) for about 100 yards to a stile, and pass behind a shed to a gate and continue across the fields, keeping right near the top of the field at first until a stile through a high hedge comes into view. Another stile is visible beyond, whence the path leads down to a gate and a farm road below. Turn left along the road and through a farmyard, and so enter the A417 just short of the Twelve Bells Inn.

114

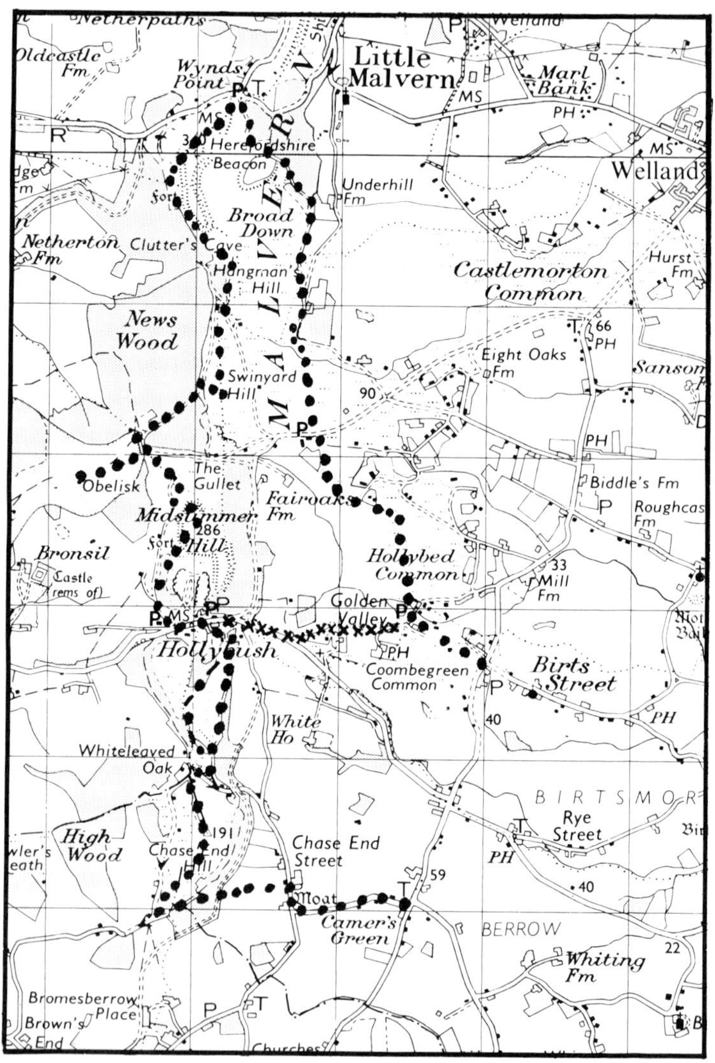

O.S. 150   ×××× link route   •—•—• alternative route

21 THE MALVERN HILLS AND COMMONS (8½ miles)

Derrick Boorne

*Travel: British Rail to Gloucester and then by Bristol Bus No. 572 to
Coombegreen Common. Return to Gloucester from Camer's Green by
same bus service or from Bromsberrow on A417 by Bristol Bus No. 573.
(There are no Sunday buses on either route.) Motorists: Car parks at
Hollybed Common; south-east of Swinyard Hill; below Herefordshire
Beacon; off A438 west and east of Hollybush.
Refreshments: British Camp Inn and Snack Bar on A449.
[Map: Ordnance Survey 1:50,000 Series, Sheet 150.]*

The Malvern Hills provide one of the finest ridge walks in England outside the mountains; they present a spectacular profile from afar, a
deservedly mini-mountain challenge. There are fortunately numerous
easy ways to avoid the challenge if desired.

The main walk starts from the bus-stop at Coombegreen Common
(G.R. 780366), but motorists can join it at several places and can complete the main circuit by using the link route between Hollybush and
Hollybed Common. Cross Coombegreen Common in a west-north-west
direction following a path which begins almost opposite the turning for
Birts Street and Birtsmorton and is roughly in line with it. One soon
arrives at a large pleasant pond on the edge of Hollybed Common with
a car parking area adjoining. You are now on part of the 2,400 acres of
common and open hill administered by the Malvern Hills Conservators,
a statutory body acting under powers given by the Malvern Hills Acts
1884-1930. The Acts charge them with the duty of preserving the hills
and commons in their natural state for the use and enjoyment of the
public, subject to the rights of Commoners.

With the pond on your left go along the dam, and then north-westwards
across Hollybed Common, following roughly the field boundary. This
leads past cottages into a wide green track which crosses a minor road
to emerge on to Castlemorton Common under the slopes of Swinyard
Hill. Cross the Common northwards (i.e. roughly parallel with the line
of the hills) making for the west side of a wood under Hangman's Hill,
and follow a track past cottages, to emerge on to a small common
(Shadybank Common). Here you must leave the track (which goes on
to Underhill Farm) and veer away from it slightly left (north-north-
westwards) along the western edge of the common. Then after climbing

gradually through woods you will come to the reservoir for Great
Malvern nestling at the foot of the hills. Follow round the northern
perimeter of the reservoir and along its access road to reach the large
car park beneath the Herefordshire Beacon (British Camp Inn, snack
bar and toilets).

It is a steep climb from the car park to the Beacon, 340 metres
(1114 ft.) and the British Camp (perhaps the best preserved of all these
ancient hill fort earthworks), but the effort is well worth it for the
splendid views in all directions. From the top, follow the ridge southwards to the circular sign-stone near Clutter's Cave. (This point can also
be reached from the car park by a good, easy lower path.) Continue
either via the cave or Hangman's Hill to Swinyard Hill. Descend in a
westerly direction to News Wood where a sometimes muddy bridle path
leads to a junction of ways on the edge of Eastnor Park. A short diversion to the Monument is worthwhile for the glorious views it affords of
the west slopes of the Malvern Hills. The monument was erected in 1812
and is inscribed to the Baron of Evesham, Lord John Somers, etc. You
are likely to see some of the large herd of red deer introduced to the
Park in 1570, but you should keep to the route marked with white
posts, in the interests of nature conservation. (Some 2 miles south-west

Herefordshire Beacon from Black Hill

of the Monument is Eastnor Castle, built in 1814 by John, first Earl
Somers. It is an excellent example of nineteenth-century castellated
architecture and contains a superb collection of armour, etc. It is open
on Sundays, Easter to September, 2.15 to 6 p.m.)

Returning to the main ridge and the junction of ways turn to the
right up a track and then left up a grassy path which leads to Mid-
summer Hill (National Trust), another splendid viewpoint. Beyond the
shelter, a path leads steeply downhill to the A438. To the left is one of
the two remaining quarries in the Malvern Hills. The Conservators have
been engaged in a long struggle to stop quarrying, which in the twenties
was so widespread that every hill was affected. The loans for the quarries'
acquisition under compulsory powers are still being repaid by the local
ratepayers, so do not begrudge any modest parking fees charged.

Turn left down the main road (A438) for 250 yards to Hollybush
post office. (Here you can, if you wish, shorten the walk by taking the
link route across to Coombegreen Common and the starting point, as
shown on the map. You will in any case need to take this route if you
have come by car and wish to complete the circuit easily. Continue
along the A438 for about a quarter of a mile to a small car park on the
common and then follow a track behind the nearby church as it runs
eastwards across Coombegreen Common. This will bring you to the
northern side of the large pond where you can rejoin the main route.)
At the post office a path starts its traverse of the east side of Ragged Stone
Hill. One can continue easily along this path to Whiteleaved Oak, but it
is better to take the right fork to the top of Ragged Stone Hill for
more excellent views, and to descend by a path to the south. Cross the
lane at Whiteleaved Oak and go up a path which leads to the Common
and to the top of Chase End Hill, the southernmost point of the
Malvern Hills, with an extensive landscape of now undulating Gloucestershire countryside stretching to distant May Hill and the Forest of
Dean.

The easy slope is followed southwards; turn left at a wall, go through
a gate, pass through two further gates and at the next (the fourth from
Common), turn right down a steepish path. Cross a good track and take
a path along the edge of a field to Gate House (marked 'Moat' on map).
Turn right along the lane and then left to Camer's Green (half a mile)
for the bus to Gloucester.

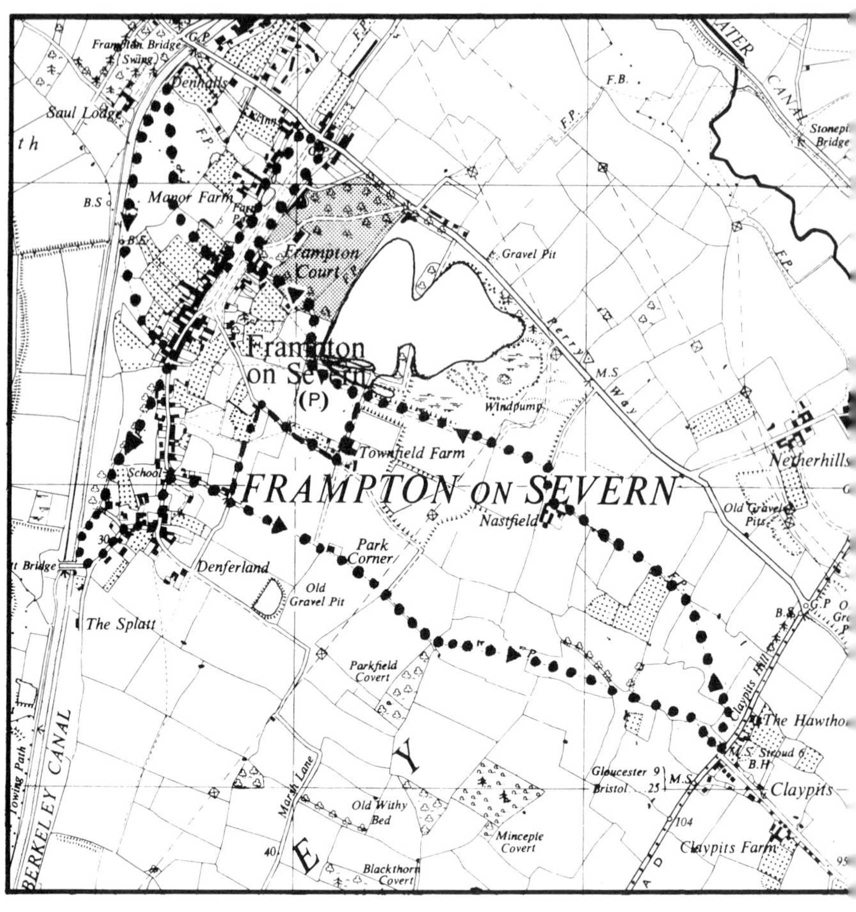

O.S. Sheet SO 70 •—•—• shorter walk

22 FRAMPTON-ON-SEVERN (5½ miles; shorter walk 3 miles)

Stephen Taylor

Travel: From Bristol or Gloucester by Bristol Bus Nos. 525/6 and 820 to Claypits Hill. From Stroud by Bristol Bus No. 416 (not Sunday mornings) to Claypits Hill. Alternatively for the shortened version of the walk take Bristol Bus No. 568 from Gloucester to Frampton-on-Severn (approximately two-hourly service and not Sundays) or Lock's Coaches service from Gloucester to Frampton Bridge (not Sundays) or Bristol Bus No. 427 from Stroud to Frampton-on-Severn (infrequent service and not Sundays). Motorists: Adequate room to park in the village, in which case the shortened version of the walk can be taken. Refreshments: Pubs in Frampton.
[Map: Ordnance Survey 1:50,000 Series, Sheet 162 or 1:25,000 Series, Sheet SO 70 (preferable).]

Unlike most of the walks in this book this one takes you over relatively flat country. There are no panoramic views on which to feast the eye, no heady, wind-swept heights to scale, yet because Frampton-on-Severn has such unique charm and special atmosphere you will discover, as I have, that walking in and around it is both attractive and enjoyable. You will find in this large village a fine selection of well-cared-for buildings of many periods flanking the huge village green, some of them cosy thatched cottages set in flower-filled gardens. You may also detect a faint nautical air to the place, since the great Gloucester and Sharpness Canal runs along its western edge, there are several lakes on its eastern edge and the nearby River Severn (a little further away from the village than the latter's name suggests) is wide enough to look at times more like a small inland sea.

This walk begins at the Claypits Hill bus-stop on the A38 (G.R. 764062). Almost opposite the turning for Eastington and Frocester climb over a stile signposted to Frampton and strike diagonally right across the field, passing the right-hand end of the first hedge you come to. The next hedge down the field contains a double stile fairly near the left boundary. Climb over this and continue across in the same half-right direction to another double stile in the far right-hand corner of the field. Climb over this and continue straight ahead now after climbing over a fence into the next field. You will eventually find yourself on a farm track cut out of the bank on your left. Notice the interesting soil profile so revealed.

Following down this track past Nastfield Farm on your left, turn right on to a new concrete farm road, and shortly afterwards turn left on to a hard track. This brings you into an area once used for gravel working and now becoming a fine place for wild life of all kinds, particularly water-fowl. There are several large stretches of water, old flooded gravel workings which have been suitably landscaped and naturalised to make pleasing additions to the landscape. One of them is on the right only a short distance from the track and is a popular place for anglers. Another one further away to the left (which you will pass on your way back to Claypits) is used for sailing.

Continue along the hard track and when it turns left towards the sailing lake go straight ahead via a stile into a field with some woodland on your right. Climb the next stile directly ahead and then turn half-right to another stile in the field boundary on the right. Turn right here over this stile and with the field boundary alongside you on your right come to yet another stile. Climb this and turn left via a cattle grid along a tarmacadam track, crossing another cattle grid soon after and passing one or two cottages. You now emerge on to the road through the village and the huge village green (the largest in Gloucestershire). Turn right and walk along the green parallel with the road. On your right you will catch a glimpse of Frampton Court, an impressive Georgian mansion, in the grounds of which is an extraordinary orangery, the white Gothic folly-like structure you can see rising above the boundary wall.

Before reaching the T-junction with the B4071 ahead cross the road to the other half of the green and double back towards the centre of the village, passing a variety of buildings of character and charm on your right. Note particularly the ancient and beautiful half-timbered Manor Farm with its fine barn and dovecote. Here was born Jane Clifford, better known as Fair Rosamund, who became the mistress of Henry II and is supposed to have been poisoned by Queen Eleanor in 1177. A little further on turn right by the side of Jones's Stores along a footpath signposted to Frampton Bridge. Climb over three stiles in succession and then bear half-right towards the canal bank. On reaching the tow-path turn right to the swing bridge and admire the spick and span condition of all the canal equipment, including the charming little white bridge-keeper's cottage with its 'mini' portico. If you are lucky you may see the bridge opened to let a ship come through. Vessels of up to 1,000 tons are able to use this canal, which

connects Gloucester with the Severn. Now turn back and walk along the
tow-path for just over half a mile, looking out for a stile set at an angle
in the hedge on your left. Climb over this and cross the field diagonally,
eventually coming out into a short lane between houses which leads
directly into the main village street.

Turn right along the latter for a very short distance and then look
out for a footpath going off at an angle on the right. This leads you
gradually towards the canal tow-path again, but, more importantly, it
takes you to Frampton Church, a building going back to the fourteenth
century and containing many interesting relics, including a fine Norman
font.

From the church it is a short walk to Splatt Bridge, another swing-
bridge over the canal with another quaint little cottage nestling beside it.
You can get a sight of the Severn now across the fields, with Slimbridge
only about a mile away to the left.

From the bridge walk back along the road for about a third of a mile
into the village and turn right along a residential road with an old school

Frampton-on-Severn

building on the corner. The road eventually becomes a track which runs along the side of the sailing lake for a while. Look out for interesting geese, duck and other water fowl on the surface of the water or feeding on the adjoining fields. Pass under some power lines and go through a bridle gate at the left-hand edge of a small copse. Continue generally straight ahead, via a succession of gates, through four pasture fields on gently rising land with the buildings at Claypits and traffic on the A38 coming into view ahead. The last lap takes you straight up to the stile to the A38 which you climbed at the start.

As you will see from the map, the shortened version of this walk omits the section between the lakes and Claypits Hill. It takes you instead by track and footpath (as shown by the dotted line) along the northern and western sides of the sailing lake.

Milton End
9
Overton
Wick
Court
Moat
Ferry
Upper
Upper
Framilode
Lea Court
Fm
PH
9 PH
P
T
Moor
Fm
12
Barrow
Hill
82
Overton
Fm
16
FRETHERNE WITH SAUL
Packthorne
Fm
10
M
V
The
Reddings
Fretherne
T
PH
7
P
Saul
Lock
Whitminster Ho
9
Hock Cliff
Wheatenhurst
8
10
Oatfield
Highfield
Ho
Whitminster
Saul Lodge
Saul
Warth
P
Frampton
Court
Frampton
on Severn
MS
18
Mill
12
The Noose

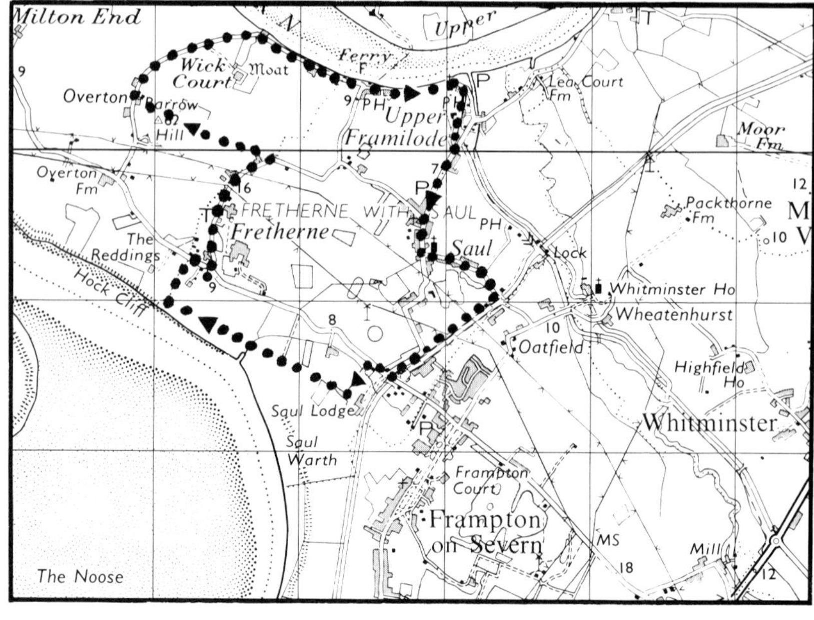

O.S. 162

23 A SEVERN PENINSULAR WALK (6½ miles)

Stephen Taylor

*Travel: From Gloucester Bus Station by Bristol Bus No. 568 (approx.
two-hourly service and not Sundays) or from Stroud Bus Station by
Bristol Bus No. 427 (infrequent and not Sundays) to northern outskirts
of Frampton-on-Severn and then walk along B4071 to Frampton
Bridge. Alternatively use Locks Coaches service from Gloucester Bus
Station to Frampton Bridge (not Sundays). From Bristol either go into
Gloucester by British Rail and then get a bus, or take Bristol Bus
Nos. 526 or 529 to Whitminster Hotel and intercept Buses 427 or 568
there. Motorists can leave cars at Frampton-on-Severn or Upper Frami-
lode or Saul.*
Refreshments: Pubs at Frampton-on-Severn, Upper Framilode and Saul.
[Map: Ordnance Survey 1:50,000 Series, Sheet 162.]

After it has passed Gloucester on its way to the sea the River Severn
indulges in a series of wild twists and turns. Perhaps its most dramatic
effort occurs in the Newnham area where it almost doubles back on
itself, leaving a tongue of land surrounded on three sides by water. Not
content with that, the river then quite suddenly increases its width to
1½ miles. This walk takes you into this strange, fascinating, watery
landscape and right across that little peninsula.

The walk begins at Frampton Bridge (G.R. 746085), the swing-
bridge over the Gloucester and Sharpness Canal, which is the most
northerly point reached on Walk No. 22. Cross the Canal north-
westwards and continue straight ahead on the road for Fretherne and
Arlingham for about 200 yards. Just past Gorway Cottage turn off left
down a track, at the end of which turn right via a hunting-gate along a
path between hedges or small trees. (At the time of writing this path
was rather overgrown, though still negotiable.) Continue along this
path in a more or less straight line and via a succession of gates and
stiles for about three-quarters of a mile, gradually coming closer and
closer to the bank of the Severn on your left. Notice that owing to the
sharp bend in the river here you are looking *along* the river rather than
across it, so that the expanse of water, particularly at high tide, appears
almost boundless. At one point along this section the path brings you
out on to the open river bank, with the field boundary on your right,
but at the next stile you must climb back inside the boundary again.

The Severn at Fretherne

Across the fields on your right you will see Fretherne Church, a remarkable ornate and imposing Victorian edifice. The land begins to rise very slightly to produce low, fossil-bearing cliffs which the river is constantly eroding. Incidentally, this is one of the places from which the Severn Bore can be seen at its best. Although the path continues north-westwards along the cliff edge you must turn away from it to begin your crossing of the peninsula. So, at the boundary between two fields negotiate a double stile and turn right, with the river behind you and a hedge on your right. Go out through the field gate and turn right along the road for about 200 yards to Fretherne Church. Whatever you may think about its architectural qualities it is worth going inside to see some of its unusual possessions.

Now walk along the minor road opposite the church for about three-quarters of a mile until you come to a farm on your left, a footpath sign to Arlingham and a sharp right-hand bend in the road just beyond. Follow the sign left through the rather muddy farmyard, past a collection of implements and go straight ahead over gently rising ground, aiming for the left-hand edge of the wood a third of a mile ahead on the lower slopes of Barrow Hill, the highest point for miles. With this wood alongside you on your right climb to the top of the hill via a small stile just beyond the wood. You now have a fence and hedge on your left and in the next field on your left there is a triangulation column. Pause awhile to admire the remarkable views of the Severn which this modest vantage point (62 metres; 203 ft.) affords. You can also enjoy fine views of the Cotswold Hills and an unusual end-on view of the Malverns. Close at hand notice that all the stones in the field appear to be smooth and rounded, obviously water-worn in the dim past when the lie of the land was very different.

Now continue straight ahead alongside the field boundary and descend the hill, crossing two stiles and passing through a small paddock, with houses on either side, to a gate opening on to a minor road. Turn right along the road, which curves gently round to the right, and in about three-quarters of a mile you will reach the bank of the Severn again. The road hugs the river bank for about three-quarters of a mile to the site of the Framilode ferry, where there is a public house, and then swings inland to Saul. However a pleasant grassy path continues beyond here along the river bank, via a white metal gate, as far as Upper Framilode Church. This stretch of the Severn seems somehow gentler and more welcoming than that on the other side of the peninsula. The river is, of course, narrower and the brisk current is thus more apparent. Away in the distance is the Forest of Dean and there is a good view of May Hill (Walk No. 24).

Walk away from the river along the road into Upper Framilode. In about 150 yards on the right you will come to the remains of the last section of the Thames–Severn Canal (see Walk No. 19). Turn right along the tow-path in front of a row of cottages flanking the canal. At the end of the row there is a handy little pub aptly named The Ship. The canal is now badly silted up but there is still enough water to enable anglers to practise their skills, and of course it makes a fine nature reserve. Rejoin the road when the canal turns underneath it and walk on into the rather sprawling village of Saul. By Saul Church a road turns off left. Go down here and in about half a mile you will come to the Gloucester and Sharpness Canal and a swing-bridge carrying the road across.

Do not cross this bridge but turn right along the tow-path instead. Soon you will draw level with a chocolate factory on the opposite bank, and if the wind is right you will have appetising smells wafted over to you to help you on the last lap of your journey. Your destination, Frampton Bridge, is just ahead.

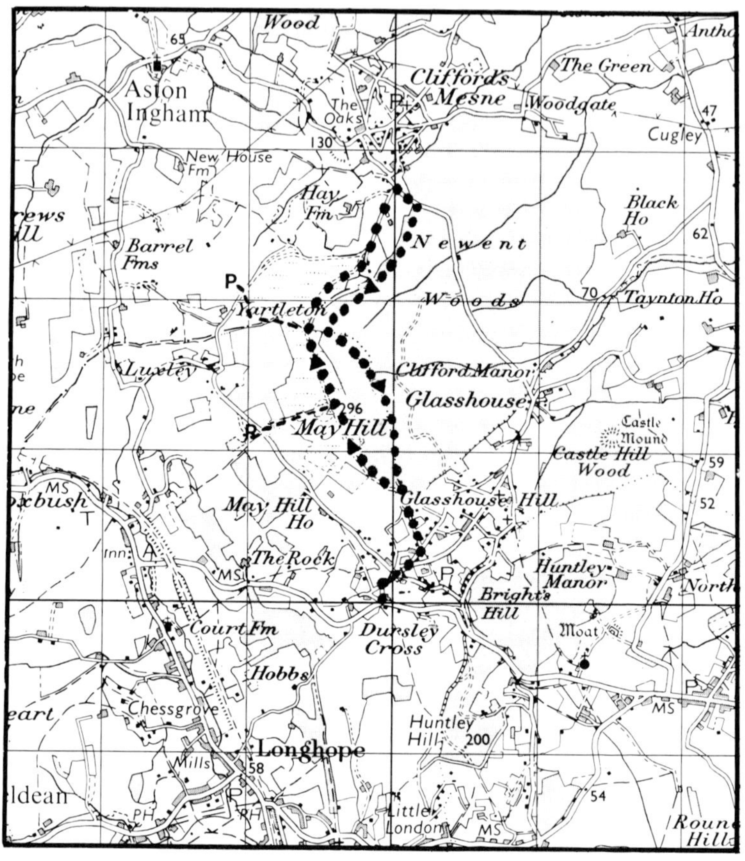

O.S. 162   — — — access routes

24 MAY HILL AND NEWENT WOODS (4 miles)

Fred Whitwood

*Travel: British Rail or Bristol Bus to Gloucester. Red and White Bus
No. 538 from Gloucester Bus Station to Dursley Cross on A40.
Motorists: Park on roadside verges west and north of May Hill.
Refreshments: Yew Tree Inn; Clifford's Mesne.
[Map: Ordnance Survey 1:50,000 Series, Sheet 162.]*

May Hill, on the northern edge of the Forest of Dean, is one of those
romantic landmarks you can see and recognise easily from a surprising
number of distant places. With its distinctive little clump of pine trees
on the very summit, somewhat reminiscent of Chanctonbury Ring on
the Sussex Downs, it stands by itself, proud and independent. At 296
metres (971 ft.) it is the highest point in Gloucestershire west of the
Severn and is therefore a splendid vantage point, giving you views in all
directions. Much of May Hill (but not the clump of trees) and some of
the surrounding woodland is owned by the National Trust.

The bus sets you down at Dursley Cross about 100 yards east of a
side road signposted 'May Hill 1' (G.R. 699200). Turn down here and
bear right at the first junction. Continue uphill and go straight over the
next cross-roads, ignoring the left-hand turning signposted to May Hill.
(Motorists, however, should turn off here to reach the parking areas,
from which there are convenient paths to link up with the main route.)
Soon after the cross-roads take the left fork and, just past the first
houses a short way up the hill, fork left again into a lane, still uphill. As
you pass an orchard on the left some good views over the Forest of
Dean can be seen beyond. The lane soon becomes a rough track which
takes you up to a large green tank on the right at a crossing of the paths.
From here take the left-hand path to a gate out on to the wide open
common and summit area with grazing for sheep and horses and
bordered by woods. This area contains a wide variety of wild life for the
careful and observant walker to enjoy, and the short fine grass makes
for pleasant walking. At the gateway a pause to look back at the con-
tortions of the River Severn, now easily visible in clear weather, should
enliven the appetite for the more extensive views from the hilltop a
little way ahead. After passing through the gate keep near the right-
hand fence at the edge of the woods. Soon the pine trees come into
view, providing a bee-line for the top.

May Hill from Framilode

May Hill, as with so many of our prominent summits, has traditional connections with early British and Roman rites, and its use for May Day festivities seems to have caused an earlier name, Yartlebury Hill, to be changed to its present one. It was also a beacon point for spreading news of the Spanish Armada's approach. The present ageing and weather-beaten plantation of pines date from 1887, Queen Victoria's Golden Jubilee, and some young replacements are now being established.

Obviously it is best to come here when visibility is good in order to enjoy and study (preferably with binoculars) the remarkable views over many adjacent counties. Clockwise, these views take in the Cotswolds and the Severn and its estuary to the east, the Forest of Dean coming almost into the foreground to the south; then as one turns westwards the distant ranges of the Black Mountains and the Sugar Loaf near Abergavenny can be made out, with the far Welsh Hills disappearing into the distance. Finally, the long humped ridge of the Malvern Hills shows up clearly to the north and north-east, and leads one's eyes round to Bredon Hill and so back to the Cotswolds.

132

Now continuing in roughly the same direction as on the approach to the summit, leave the pines on your left and begin the long descent towards the village of Clifford's Mesne along a clear grass track. This passes through a field gate near the corner of Newent Woods running along on your right. Note the clumps of broom growing on either side of the track as it descends more steeply. Eventually you will come to a minor road or track: bear right along it past (or into) the Yew Tree Inn (on your left). Soon after this turn right into a more substantial road and in about 300 yards enter Newent Woods by the first clear path off on your right, just past a gate into a field.

The woods contain some particularly fine specimens of native hardwoods and some more unusual conifers. Needless to say, the warning notices you will encounter about the dangers of fire must be taken very seriously. In the late spring there are great drifts of bluebells under the trees to delight the eye. Amongst other interesting things you will come across from time to time are heaped mounds of conifer needles containing the nests of large wood ants.

Keep to the right-hand main route running more or less parallel with the edge of the woods until you reach a gate leading on to the common. Here take the highest path ahead which leads up to the inside corner of the wood near the gate through which you passed on the way down from the summit. Do not leave the woods yet, however, but turn left on to a path which soon broadens out into a substantial track. At junctions along this track keep to the right to emerge into an open section and cross a fenced area with stiles on each side. A short distance beyond this, at a general meeting of paths, take the right-hand track down to the large green tank you passed on the way up. From here you simply retrace your steps back to the bus-stop, or, if you have come by car, turn right and go back over the hill to the parking area.

Hale Woods
Cairn
Inn Tintern Parva
Oakhill Wood
Fire Tower
ERN
Barbadoes Hill
Caswell Wood
Offa's Dyke Path
Madgetts Fm
Weir
Buckle Wood
Offa's
197
Chapel Hill
Hotel
Sheepcot
Chase Ho
237
Tintern Abbey
MS
Weir
Devil's Pulpit
214
Penterry Fm
Reddings Fm
High Wood
The
217
Park
Banton
Sharp Cliff
Poor
Fort
Linen Well
Cairn
Chase Fm
MS
w Wood
Weir
WT Sta
Weir
James's Thorns
Tidenham Chase
Black Cliff
RIVER
Quarry
Parson's Allotment
Porthcasseg
Weir
260
G der Hill
Enclosure
WYE
235
Wyndcliffe Court
Wynd Cliff
Livox Fm
Dennel Hill
Prior's Reach
Weir
MS
93
Weir
Offa's Dyke Path
Lover's Leap
Weir
Fort
117 Ashberry Ho
Philpot Court
Lancaut
40
Church
Cross Hill
St Arvans
P
Wintour's Leap
Hotel
MS
Weir
Broadrock
101
Oakgrove
Piercefield
Fort
Woodcroft
48
Cliffs
Weir
MS
Race Course
Piercefield Park
Longhope Reach
111
Fryth Wood
Grandstands
Tutshill
82
MS
Snipehill Br
A Crossway Green
MS
55
Tump Fm
MS
Earthwork
72
Castle
Great Barnets Woods
CHEPSTOW
Badams Court
Hospl
Sedbury
Sewage Works
Wks
Sedbury School
78
28

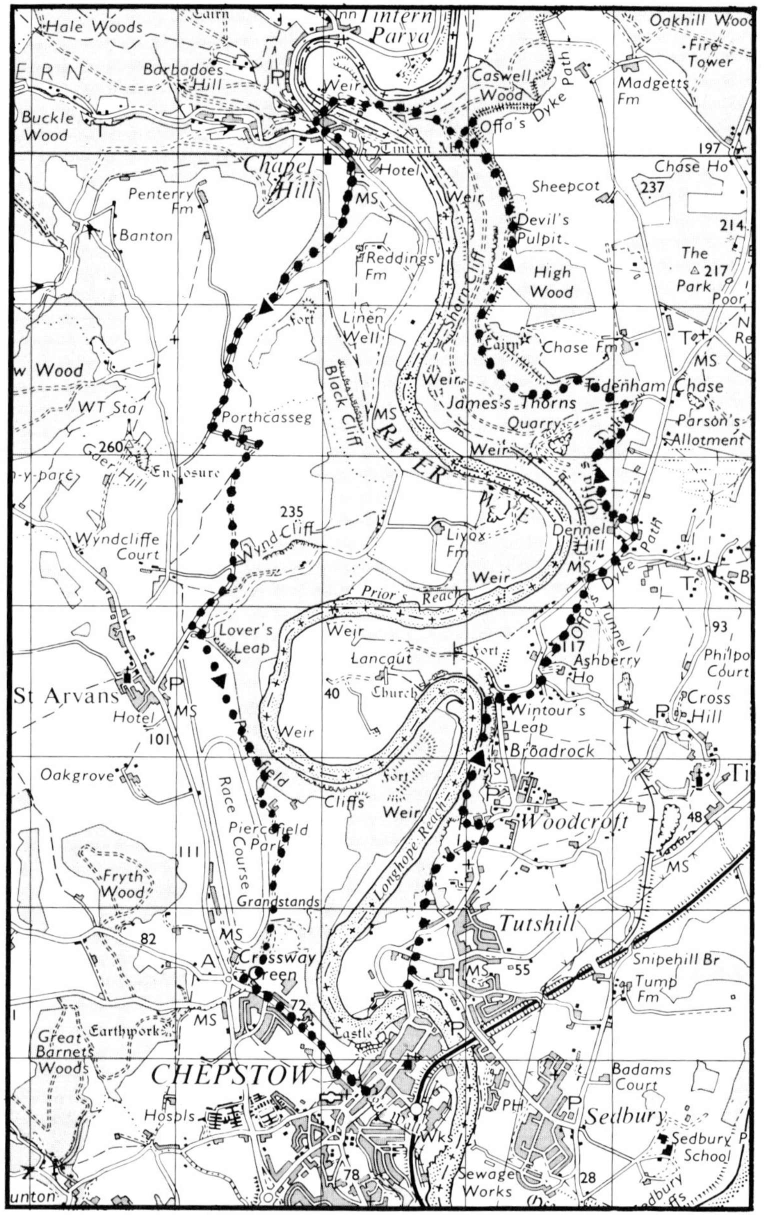

O.S. 162

25 THE LOWER WYE AND OFFA'S DYKE (9 miles; shorter walk 5 miles)

Ian Campbell

Travel: Bristol Bus No. 300 from Bristol to Chepstow (via Severn Bridge). Mainly 2 hourly service weekdays and Sundays. Return same route. Motorists: Park in Chepstow or Tintern.
Refreshments: Tintern and Chepstow.
[Map: Ordnance Survey 1:50,000 Series, Sheet 162.]

For the first part of this walk we follow part of Offa's Dyke Path — the long-distance route which stretches from the Severn near Chepstow to the coast of North Wales. For two or three miles on our route the path runs on top of, or immediately alongside, the Dyke itself.

Offa, who reigned in the late eighth century, was the king of Mercia, an area comprising a rough square with Chepstow, Chester, Lincoln and St Albans as its four corners. For the previous two centuries the English had been slowly advancing westwards, pushing the Britons before them. by Offa's reign, the Britons were in their last strongholds — Wales and Cornwall. Offa fought a series of wars against the Britons, but he soon came to the conclusion that further advance into the barren hills of Wales would be both unrewarding and militarily expensive. His main political ambitions switched in the 780s to extending Mercia southwards at the expense of other English kingdoms. Hence he sought to end the wars with the Britons, or Welsh as they were coming to be called, and to delimit the frontier. The result was Offa's Dyke, an earthwork which marked the border between England and Wales for centuries. Even today the modern boundary still approximates to Offa's Dyke. The Dyke seems to have been a negotiated boundary line rather than a defensive work like Hadrian's Wall, but it is easy to see which was the stronger power: even on our short stretch all the main views are to the westward, i.e. into Wales, and this is the pattern throughout its length.

To reach the Dyke from Chepstow bus station, walk through the town to the bridge which carries the A48 road to Gloucester across the Wye. On the other side continue straight up the steep lane, cross the main road at the top and continue for a few yards down the B4228. Shortly a stile is reached on the left with the Countryside Commission acorn displayed, the sign of a long-distance route. On the right of the

135

path is the ruined Tutshill Tower. This of course has nothing to do with Offa, and was erected as a beacon in Henry VIII's time. A fragment of the Dyke is visible on the left — a small earth bank. On the other side of the field, cross the stile and follow the path alongside a park wall; at the far end turn left, then almost immediately right on to a driveway. Halfway along, the path leaves the driveway by a stile and crosses a field. Turn right down a track to the B4228 again. Twenty yards further on the path leaves the road by a sharp V-turn under an arch and winds up to go alongside the Lancourt quarries. There is a magnificent view across the horseshoe bend of the Wye to the towering cliffs of Wyndcliffe on the far side. The Dyke itself is entirely lost here; possibly it ran nearer the river on land later quarried away. It is now necessary to walk for a hundred yards or so along the B4228 until Offa's Dyke Farm. Leave the road on the right by a stone stile opposite the farm. Crossing the field, the general rule of this walk is broken and there are superb views to the eastward, over the Severn estuary, and the triangular-shaped reservoir at Oldbury-on-Severn, built in the estuarial mud, is clearly visible. At the end of the field we re-enter the B4228 for the last time and then, after a couple of hundred yards, leave it by a path on the left, just before a derelict cottage. After a short distance through scrub, the path turns right on to the Dyke itself.

The next couple of miles is superb walking, with glances of the river below and the Welsh hills beyond. The path and Dyke are very easy to follow and keep pretty well to the 600-foot contour line, except when both dip down to cross a minor dry valley coming in from the right. After about a mile and a half, the Devil's Pulpit is reached, with a magnificent view of Tintern Abbey nestling by the river below. Legend had it that the Devil had an abode hereabout, from whence he used to harangue the monks below and try to seduce them from their allegiance.

The path continues at the foot of the Dyke, which is here a massive earthwork, possibly because the Wye valley broadens and there was probably a Welsh settlement on the rich soils below which needed watching. After half a mile the path turns right and cuts through the Dyke, and this enables the scale of the earthwork to be appreciated. The serfs from miles around — as well no doubt as Welsh prisoners — must have been pressed into service for many a weary month.

At this point we leave the Dyke and turn left down the zig-zag path to Tintern. There are good views southwards down the Wye Valley to the Severn estuary beyond.

Tintern Abbey well repays a visit. It was founded in 1131 as an Abbey of the Cistercian Order and built according to their rule — in quiet places, away from Norman towns and castles. Tintern has managed to preserve its beauty in this spot,and in the season it attracts many visitors. The Abbey was dissolved by Henry VIII in 1536 and the lead from its roofs melted down. Thereafter it remained in the hands of Dukes of Beaufort until sold to the Crown early in this century. It is now managed by the Department of the Environment.

Those who wish to end their walk here can do so, on weekdays, by catching Red and White Service 50 (approx. hourly) back to Chepstow from outside the Abbey. Note that this bus service, like other things in Wales, does not operate on Sundays.

If you have time and energy, however, continue the walk back to Chepstow on the Welsh side of the river. Cross the road opposite the entrance to the Abbey and go up the lane. Turn sharp left and follow it as it bends right up the small wooded valley. Do not be tempted by the acorn signpost leading off to the left, but keep straight on. At the top a metalled farm road comes in from the right. Follow this, turning left to Porthcasseg Farm. Past the farm buildings turn right through a white gate, and follow the path across a pasture field until it joins a minor road at Wyndcliffe. There are excellent views across the river to Lancourt where we were a few hours earlier. Indeed, someone in the County Planning Department has been so impressed with the view that

Chepstow Castle

this spot has been officially designated a 'viewpoint' — though the practical effect of such designation is difficult to see.

Follow the minor road downhill and cross the A466 at the bottom. We are now in Piercefield Park, the site of Chepstow Race Course. The path keeps to the grass to the left of the track, with the grandstand away to the right. Past the race track the path comes into the road in the outskirts of Chepstow, about half a mile from the Castle.

If you have time before your bus goes, Chepstow and its Castle are well worth exploring and there are, of course, a number of excellent hostelries.

One of the most intriguing things about Chepstow is its name. Although firmly on the Welsh side both of the Wye and of Offa's Dyke, it has a distinctly Saxon name (Chepe = market, Stow = town). Historians are divided on the answer. Possibly Offa had a bridgehead on this bank for trade? At any rate, Chepstow was a thriving market town throughout the Saxon and Norman period and only declined in fairly modern times with the rise of Newport, Avonmouth and Cardiff.

The Garth
68
MS
Highmeadow
Woods
175
Coalpit
Hill
Christ
225
P
Staunton
May Hill
Kymin
T
Naval
Temple
Buck
Stone
202
Twr
279
Marian
Inclosure
Wyesham
Staunton
Meend
MS
Wks
Offa's
Cse of old rly
208
Birchen
Wood
Bunjups
Wood
Crossways
Lord's
Grove
Path
Dyke
Knockalls
Inclosure
P
Scowl
T
P
MS
P
MS
Penallt
Park
ood
High
Meadow
Quarry
130
MS
Redbrook
P
Newland
Glyn
Fm
P
Cse of old rly
Pen-
garn
Inn
Lower
Redbrook
Mill
P
PH
Pent-
twyn
Highbury
Fm
MS
roft
Penallt
Sewage

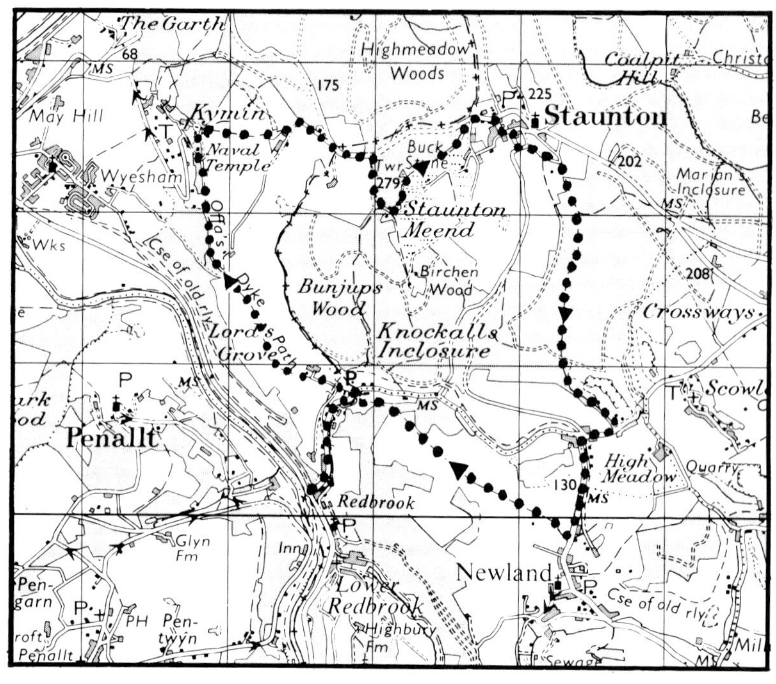

O.S. 162

26 TO THE KYMIN AND INTO THE FOREST OF DEAN
(7 miles)

Kenneth Pinnock

Travel: Bristol Bus No. 300 from Bristol Bus Station to Chepstow, thence Red and White Bus No. 49 to Redbrook. Motorists: A useful spot for car parking is at G.R. 538108 beside the B4231 Redbrook-Lydney road, about 50 yards beyond the lane on the left, marked by an Offa's Dyke Path sign, which is the real beginning of the walk. Refreshments: Ample in Redbrook. Inns at Staunton and Newland. [Map: Ordnance Survey 1:50,000 Series, No. 162.]

On this ramble we go along a stretch of the Offa's Dyke long-distance footpath from Redbrook in the Wye Valley as far as the curious Naval Temple on the Kymin, above Monmouth. We then strike eastwards into the Forest of Dean towards the Buckstone and the village of Staunton. Attractive and easy forest paths take us on to Newland, with its large and lovely 'Cathedral of the Forest'. The final stretch is by quiet field-paths back to Redbrook.

Alight from the bus at Redbrook on the A466, walk from the Bush Inn up the B4231 for half a mile and then turn left along the lane marked by an Offa's Dyke Path sign. This sunken rising track opens out at the top to become a metalled road as far as a farm, whence it becomes rough again. White-painted acorns (long-distance path way-marks) or arrows on stiles mark the way through the fields to the Kymin, a steep hill overlooking Monmouth. This is National Trust land, and here will be found the Naval Temple built in 1800 'to perpetuate the names of those noble Admirals who distinguished themselves by their Glorious Victories for England in the last and present Wars'. Here is also the Round House (1794), once a pavilion or summer house, a relic of the days when the Kymin was a pleasure ground for the gentry of Monmouth. From here, if visibility is good, the Black Mountains and the Brecon Beacons can be seen as a backdrop to the almost aerial view over Monmouth.

Leave the Kymin along the path to the left of the Round House (i.e. with your back towards Monmouth) to a stile in an angle of the hedge. Now strike across the field, making for a gap well to the right of a barn, and so along a clearer cart track down to a house and stile to the left of the farm at G.R. 534126. Again, if visibility is good, there are

fine views to be had as you cross this field, including the Malvern Hills
away to the left, with the television mast on Ridge Hill, 20 miles away.
Climb the above-mentioned stile, and follow the road left and so reach
the main A4136 road in a quarter of a mile.

Carry on along this road for about 250 yards to leave it by a narrow
path on the right just in front of the Forestry Commission sign, ascending rapidly before emerging on a wide crossing track at the top. Turn
right, and fork left soon after, walking under electric cables to arrive at
the Adventure Centre. Here turn left, and left again at a red-brick
house, to follow a rising narrow path through bracken, parallel to a
stone wall. Over a stile at the top is the famous Buckstone, which used
to rock until dislodged in 1885. This is an ideal place for a picnic.

Turning left from the stile, continue down towards Staunton on the
waymarked path, turning left at the bottom, and soon afterwards right
to enter the village. Turn right just past the Inn, along the Newland/
Redbrook road, which you now follow as far as the second right bend

Staunton

at G.R. 550125. Leave the road here, and go left along a rough track which becomes narrower and grassy as it approaches the crossing at its end. Here turn right along a wider track into woodland. Soon at the crossing of paths, ignore the more obvious one which goes straight ahead, and is not shown on the Ordnance Survey Map. Instead, follow the right fork to the second crossing in half a mile, ignoring all other side tracks. Again, note that the first crossing is not shown on the Ordnance Survey Map. Cross straight over on a narrow, descending path through the trees. (When this walk was prepared, the start of this path was obscured by a fallen tree, and so can be easily missed.) Turn left at the bottom on to a wider track, and so come to a minor road near a quarry entrance.

Turn right along this road, then turn left at the road junction along the B4231 to Newland. Do not fail to visit Newland Church, the 'Cathedral of the Forest'. This beautiful and impressive building goes back to the thirteenth century and contains many interesting relics and monuments. On leaving the church retrace your steps northwards along the B4231 until you come to a footpath on the left signposted 'Upper Redbrook', at a stile opposite a white house on the outskirts of the village. From the stile, follow the path as it veers over towards a hedge, and then runs alongside it through the first 1½ fields. Now go over a gate, and continue along the path in the same direction but now along the *right*-hand edges of four more fields. Notice the charred stump in the middle of the field adjoining the first. This is all that remains of the Newland Great Oak, which, before it was struck by lightning in 1955, was the largest oak tree in the country, with a girth of 40 feet. In the third field, there is a large and very muddy patch in the corner. You can avoid the worst of this by bearing left after the gate along a curving cart track to a gap in the facing hedge. If you do this return to the proper line of walking as soon as possible, to keep on the right of way. From the corner stile, follow the left fence to another stile at the tip of the wood at G.R. 543106. Now cross the large field to a hidden stile in the edge of the wood on the far side, making for a point some 50 yards left of an electricity pole. Follow the obvious narrow track down through the wood to the fence at the end, clambering over it to enter the field ahead. Cross this in the same direction to the facing stile on the far side, and continue thence along a narrow track and over a footbridge, to rejoin the road, right opposite the starting point.

Rhyd-y-maen
Wern
Duffryr
25
89
99
80 P
Llansoy
110
100
Inn
29
Gwernesney
56
Pill Brook
Cwrty
Brychan
Slough
MS
Llangwm-isaf
Fm
Llar
Cou
56
49
134
Ringwork
Lan-pill
Woods
Llan-pill
40
110
Llangwm-isaf
y-bach
Wern
Birs
P
PH
Llangwm
Earthwork
Nantygelli
Fm
Wolvesnewton
Ringwork
Gr
Pentwyn
House Fm
Cefnbychan
Moat
wnwr
158
Nant-y-
march
Cae
Pwtto
Cw
Fort
130
8
MS
New
Ho
Model
Fm
Gaer-fawr
KILGWRRV

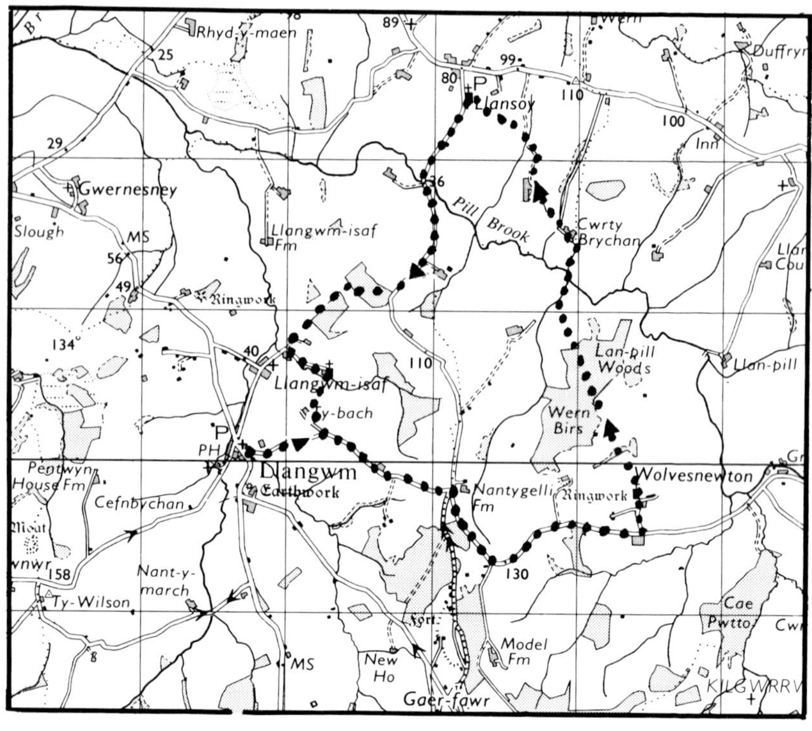

O.S. 171

27 A GWENT GEM (7 miles)

Kenneth Pinnock

Travel: Bristol Bus No. 300 from Bristol to Chepstow. Thence Red and White Bus No. 119 to Llangwm, Bridge Inn (two-hourly service and not Sundays). Motorists: Limited parking in Llangwm, or at Bridge Inn, by arrangement with inn-keeper.
Refreshments: Bridge Inn.
[Map: Ordnance Survey 1:50,000 Series, Sheet 171.] (N.B. Some of the paths used on this walk are not shown on the map. This is noted in the text.)

This is a journey to see the exquisite carved rood loft and screen in St Jerome's Church at Llangwm, Gwent. We reach it by a cross-country walk along quiet lanes and field-paths through some lovely unspoilt countryside.

Alight from the bus in Llangwm on the B4235 (G.R. 427002) and walk back in the direction of Chepstow for about 150 yards, until you come to the turning for Wolvesnewton and Cobblers Plain. This is on the same side of the road as the Bridge Inn. Go up this minor road and in about half a mile bear right as the access road to Ty Bach Kennels comes in on the left. Continue along the road for a further three-quarters of a mile to a T-junction, where you turn half-right, following the sign for Wolvesnewton. Soon you will pass the clearly signposted turning on the right for the small but interesting Folk Museum at Model Farm. If you have time you can divert half a mile to see this.

On reaching the outskirts of the tiny village of Wolvesnewton turn left opposite a farm and just before two modern white houses, along the dead-end road to the church. Climb the stone stile behind the church to enter the adjacent field, and follow the cart track alongside the left edge of the field for a short distance before entering the next field on the left via a wooden hand-gate. Now cut across right to, and through, the strip of woodland at G.R. 453001, to rough pasture on the other side. The way ahead is now not clear, but aim for a point about 20-25 yards to the right of a derelict cottage at the edge of the wood-land ahead. Here will be found at the end of the hedge a broken stile by a tree (G.R. 452003). The route of the path through Lan-Pill Woods is clear when found, but is misaligned from that shown on the map, coming out at a field gate right at the tip at G.R. 449008. Cross the field diagonally right past an old stone barn (not shown on the map) to a field gate in the facing hedge. Cross the next field slightly left, and cross the stream below it via an old stone bridge. Here turn right to a stile at a second bridge, this time over the Pill Brook, at G.R. 449012, and go on ahead to Brychan Farm. Turn left inside the yard, then, ignoring the farm service road in front of the house, go ahead through the facing gate into the field, and follow the right hedge up to a stile located a few yards left of the field gate in the top right corner. Climb this stile, and go left to another set of farm buildings in a few yards.

We now need to get to Llansoy Church. The path shown on the map is not easy to find, but an acceptable alternative is to follow the service road to the right to the bend just past where it crosses the stream. Go through the right hand one of two field gates, and follow the obvious cart track along the left edge of the first field to a gate set at an angle. From here follow the right hedges through two more fields to the church, which is well worth a visit if you have the time. Now turn left into an attractive country road and follow it for one mile to a wood on the left, which you enter through a facing gate set back from the road. Follow the narrow path through, which will probably be muddy but quite passable. Again, this path is not shown on the map. From the hand-gate at the top, cross the field diagonally right to a line of trees, which you now follow left, soon continuing with a new fence to a gate in the corner. Proceed straight across the next field to an open gateway at the bend of the road at G.R. 430008. (The Bridge Inn, and buses back to Chepstow, are half a mile along to the right, past the other Llangwm Church — St John's — which you can see.) Now turn left down a narrow road to reach at the end your goal of St Jerome's Church. Its marvellous rood loft and screen date from the fifteenth century, and must be seen and studied to be really appreciated. The church contains several other notable items, including an unusual stone lamp, said to date from the late eleventh century. It is salutary to realise that this is twice as old as the rood screen! The whole setting of the church in its dell by the stream is one of complete peace and tranquillity.

From the church door go through the wicket gate opposite and cross the stream just below it into the meadow.* Climb the steep slope of the

---

*At the time of writing the footbridge over the stream was out of action. If you find that it has not yet been repaired, an alternative route to the meadow is to go out of the churchyard gate, follow the sunken cart track to the right into a field, bear right and then climb over a field gate and so enter the meadow.

The rood screen, St. Jerome's Church

meadow to a hand-gate in the facing hedge, noting as you go the expanding views of the Black Mountains beyond the church. To the south, in the direction in which you are climbing, is Wentwood and the extensive pasture lands of Gwent. Continue across the next field to a white field gate, to join the access road to Ty Bach Kennels. Turn left along this and shortly afterwards turn sharp right, to join the road to Llangwm and the bus back to Chepstow.

THE CONTRIBUTORS

Kate Ashbrook is a keen walker and conservationist. She has recently obtained a degree in biology from Exeter University.

Derrick Boorne is on the staff of the Countryside Commission at Cheltenham. He is a very experienced walker and climber and a former Secretary of the London Mountaineering Club. His other interests are canoeing and back-packing.

Ian Campbell is a barrister. He was Secretary of the Commons, Open Spaces and Footpaths Preservation Society from 1964 to 1975 and is now a Vice-President.

Philip Daniell is on the staff of the British Waterways Board. His hobby is walking tow-paths, sometimes leading parties of enthusiasts on canal explorations. He is also active in local footpath groups in Bromley, Kent, where he lives.

Tony Drake is Footpaths Secretary for the Ramblers' Association, Gloucestershire Area.

Tony Jones is now Countryside Interpretive Officer for Gloucestershire County Council. In 1970 he was in charge of the Countryside Commission's nation-wide Rights of Way Survey for Schools project.

Harold Overton is a retired Librarian/Information worker. He is Secretary of the Bristol Local Group of the Ramblers' Association and was founder Secretary of the West of England Ramblers' Federation (later Ramblers' Association, West of England Area).

Bill Parfitt is a retired school-teacher and an active member of the Ramblers' Association and the Folk House Rambling Club (Bristol). He is a former chairman of the latter.

Kenneth Pinnock is a very experienced walker who for many years now has been writing a weekly ramble for the Bristol Evening Post under the pen-name of John Walker.

Dennis Thoms is a Chartered Electrical Engineer and an active member of the Ramblers' Association, Bristol Avon Area. In 1975 he established the Gordano Footpath Group.

Cyril Trenfield is County of Avon Footpaths Secretary for the Ramblers' Association. He is also a member of the Cotswolds AONB Warden Service and is Chairman of their South Cotswolds District.

Kathleen Wiggins is a solicitor working in local government. She is a keen walker and has close family ties with Somerset and Avon.

Fred Whitwood is on the staff of the Countryside Commission. He is a very experienced walker and an amateur naturalist.

General Editor:

Stephen Taylor is a civil servant specialising in countryside subjects. From 1965 to 1975 he was on the staff of the National Parks Commission and the Countryside Commission, where he concentrated on the creation of long-distance footpaths and bridleways. He is now Clerk of the Commons Commissioners.

THE COMMONS, OPEN SPACES AND FOOTPATHS PRESERVATION SOCIETY

150

This Society was founded in 1865. Its founders were conscious of the need to provide open spaces and access to the countryside for the rapidly growing urban population. It was the first organisation to be concerned with the environment. Today it has over 500 local Footpath and Commons Societies affiliated, as well as some 1,500 private individual members, and is supported by over 1,000 local authorities. Further information is obtainable from the Society's offices at 166 Shaftesbury Avenue, London WC2 8JH.

THE RAMBLERS' ASSOCIATION

The Association has nearly 30,000 individual members and over 440 affiliated rambling clubs. It is the representative organisation for anyone who enjoys a walk in the country, whether they want to complete the Pennine Way, do a gentle eight miles with the local rambling club, or walk on their own, or with friends, whether they use public or private transport.

The Association's main job is to secure and maintain the right to walk in the countryside whether on public paths or over open moorland and mountain. Secondly, it is deeply involved in the struggle to defend the countryside against encroachment. It played a major part in securing the legislation which established National Parks and the definitive mapping of footpaths, and it helped to obtain major improvements in the Countryside Act of 1968.

Its 29 Area organisations are responsible for activities throughout Britain. They look after footpaths, access problems and amenity issues in their territories as well as organising rambles and social events. In addition the Association has 139 local groups who provide an even nearer-to-home focus for activities within the Areas.

Full particulars may be obtained from The Ramblers' Association, 1/4 Crawford Mews, York Street, London W1H 1PT.

THE COUNTRYSIDE COMMISSION

The Commission is an independent statutory agency operating throughout England and Wales (there is a separate Countryside Commission for Scotland). Their three main tasks are to promote:

(a)   the conservation and enhancement of landscape beauty;
(b)   facilities for informal recreation in the countryside;
(c)   better public access to rural areas for open-air enjoyment.

By encouraging and helping to finance the provision of what people want for informal recreation — country parks, picnic sites, access to open country — the Commission can relieve pressure on the vulnerable spots already chosen for their scenic excellence — the National Parks, Areas of Outstanding Natural Beauty and Heritage Coasts. By helping better planning and management of leisure in the countryside as a whole it should be easier to look after and reconcile the different interests of those who live and work there.

One important way of promoting and improving the range of opportunities to enjoy the countryside and open-air recreation in it is by the provision and management of footpaths. Until recently the Commission's duties in this field were confined to the creation of long-distance routes to enable the public 'to make extensive journeys on foot, horseback or by bicycle'. The Local Government Act 1974 extended the Commission's range of duties, which means, among other things, that it can now help with expenditure on all footpaths for recreation.

More information, including leaflets on the various long-distance routes, may be obtained from The Countryside Commission, John Dower House, Crescent Place, Cheltenham, Glos. GL50 3RA.

BRISTOL OMNIBUS COMPANY LTD.

Bristol	290103
Bath	64446
Cheltenham	22021
Chippenham	2863
Cirencester	3004
Gloucester	27516
Stroud	3421/2
Trowbridge	3170
Wells	73084
Weston-super-Mare	21201

Head Office: Berkeley House, Lawrence Hill, Bristol BS5 ODZ.

RED AND WHITE SERVICES LTD.

Chepstow	2947
Cinderford	22196
Lydney	2734
Monmouth	2464/5

Head Office: 253 Cowbridge Road West, Ely, Cardiff, CF5 5XX.

WESTERN NATIONAL OMNIBUS CO. LTD.

Bridgwater	2136
Taunton	2033-5

Head Office: National House, Queen Street, Exeter EX4 3TF.

P.G. & M.D. LOCK

Saul	244

Head Office: Hillview Garage, Eastington, Stonehouse, Glos.

BRITISH RAIL

Bristol	294255

Bath and
Chippenham   Bath 63075
Bridgwater and
Taunton   Taunton 83444
Cheltenham,
Gloucester and
Stroud   Gloucester 29501
Weston-super-Mare   21131

PRINCIPAL SOURCES OF TOURIST INFORMATION

Avon, Somerset, Wiltshire   —   West Country Tourist Board
                                          Trinity Court
                                          Southernhay East
                                          Exeter EX1 1QS

Gloucestershire, Hereford &   —   Heart of England Tourist Board
Worcester   P.O. Box 15
                                          Worcester WR1 2JT

Gwent   —   Wales Tourist Board
                                          Welcome House
                                          Llandaff
                                          Cardiff CF5 2YZ